I Can Hear the Cowbells Ring

by
Lionel G. García

Arte Público Press
Houston, Texas
1994

This book is made possible through support from the National Endowment for the Arts (a federal agency), the Lila Wallace-Reader's Digest Fund and the Andrew W. Mellon Foundation.

Recovering the past, creating the future

Arte Público Press
University of Houston
Houston, Texas 77204-2090

Cover design by Bette Margolis

García, Lionel G.
    I can hear the cowbells ring / by Lionel G. García.
        p.   cm.
    ISBN 1-55885-114-3 : $9.95
    1. García, Lionel G.—Childhood and youth. 2.
Mexican Americans—Texas—Social life and customs.
3. Authors, American—20th century—Biography. 4.
Mexican American authors—Texas—Biography. 5.
Mexican American families—Texas. I. Title.
PS3557.A1115Z47   1994
813'.54—dc20   94-8658
    [B]   CIP

The paper used in this publication meets the requirements of the American National Standard for Permanence of Paper for Printed Library Materials Z39.48-1984. ∞

To my mother, Marillita;

my father, Gonzalo;

my grandmother, María;

my grandfather, Gonzalo;

Juan; Matías; Cota;

Maggie; Frances

Acknowledgments

"The Ringing of the Bell" first appeared in a shorter form as "Ringing of the Bell Never Ends" in *Texas Magazine, Houston Chronicle*. It was later included in the anthology, *This Place of Memory*, University of North Texas Press. It also appears in a collection by Texas A&M Press.

"Confession" first appeared in a different form in *Texas Magazine, Houston Chronicle*.

"Baseball" appeared as published in the *Texas Magazine, Houston Chronicle*.

"Tío Nano" appeared in a different form as "Table Manners" in *Texas Monthly Magazine*.

"Boxing" first appeared in a shorter form in *Texas Magazine, Houston Chronicle,* as "Punching the Bag of Happiness."

Contents

I Can Hear the Cowbells Ring

Author's Introduction
The Ringing of the Bell

I was born and raised in San Diego, Texas, the county seat of Duval County. The long years of political turmoil have covered the little town like a black cloud. To those of you not familiar with its history, the town has a reputation for being bad. It was the county seat for political shenanigans dating back to the late 1800's. This is the courthouse where the infamous Box Thirteen from neighboring Jim Wells County was burned making Lyndon Johnson a Texas senator. This is where the Parr family ruled politically for decades. This is where State Officials sent four Rangers to live, giving up on the old adage of "one riot, one ranger." This is where State Officials who came down to investigate after one election could not help but be amazed when they discovered that the people had all voted in alphabetical order.

In my very early years we were an inseparable collection of eight children brought together to gain the protection of the pack. Of course we had a pecking order. I was the youngest and the least important. If any errand needed to be run, I ran it. If any disagreeable task needed to be performed, I was chosen. My brother Richard came after me, and then my sister Sylvia—they were above me, but not by much. Then came my grandmother's children, my uncles Juan and Matías, the two dominant males. Then came my aunts Cota (Eloisa), Maggie, and Frances. Of the three aunts, Cota was the most dominant, and she fought often over leadership with her two brothers. The two branches of the family lived next to each other, separated by an empty lot.

We walked the hot, dusty, streets barefooted, our pockets full of marbles, spinning tops, mesquite sticks and balls, looking for a game to play. We were carefree then, getting up in the morning, leaving home after breakfast and not returning until dark, all dirty and sweaty, hoping some supper had been left for us.

As we crossed the yard by the light of the moon between my grandmother's house and ours, we could hear the voices of our elders, sitting on the porch at my grandmother's, my grandmother fanning herself, to shed the intense heat which had consumed her in the kitchen the whole day. By now she had annoited her arms and neck with camphorated alcohol, and the vapors of the camphor reached us from afar. Under the stars and amid the sounds of the locusts, our elders made beautiful talk about people alive or long dead.

Whenever there was disagreement as to a date, we would run to get Mercé, our insane uncle, who knew exactly when each member of the family present and gone was born. Mercé was an alcoholic and most of the time we could find him drunk, asleep in the semidarkness of his room, the lantern barely lit. Thrown on the bed, his clothes still on, snoring, the room reeking of tobacco and beer, he would have difficulty getting up, but he'd come. He loved company. If we didn't find him when we ran back home, our elders would say that Mercé was at a tavern, putting on his show of madness in exchange for a bottle of beer.

When Mercé was young he was sent to the insane asylum in San Antonio. There, in no time at all according to my grandmother, he memorized most of the streets in the city. If in the course of a conversation he had a fit, they would just let him go running through the streets as though nothing had happened. "Be careful," my grandmother would tell him. "Don't run into anything in the dark." Mercé would be gone, lost for the night. We would see him again the next morning, that is, if we didn't go sleep at his house.

It was easy to laugh and cry in the dark with the stories.

We never knew who would be there for the evening. Relatives of all shapes and forms—both physical and mental—would come. Some would stay until my grandmother couldn't keep her eyes open, others just long enough to take advantage of a free meal. Others would just happen by the street and join us. There was nothing quite so thrilling as to see a favorite storyteller approach. We knew we were in for a wonderful night of listening to tales of someone dying, dead, married, pregnant, jobless, toothless, penniless. The whole of human condition was played before our eyes and ears daily. I never realized until later how much of life I had witnessed or been revealed to me during those years.

I was raised amidst insanity with my uncle Mercé who loved me as a child and took me with him everywhere. I remember how his fits would start, sensing his changing mood, how with one hand he would yank at his ears because he heard voices that ordered him to curse and who to curse dragging me with the other around town. Some days, while he held me in his arms and took off with me, I felt there would be no end to his fits and that we were forever destined to pull at our ears and curse at the whole town. With Mercé, reality became an illusion for me. Then there was my aunt Pepa, also insane. Pepa took me by the hand, walking the streets in the daylight with a lantern like Diogenes, searching not for an honest man but for her dead husband and children. She would ask me if I could see them and I would lie and say that I could. We would then hurry to greet the apparition. The disappointment of not finding them was always followed by a smile, because she would try again in a few moments, and there would always be tomorrow. Pepa lived for tomorrow. "Tomorrow," she would say to me, "they will come." After a while I too could see her husband on horseback riding toward us. Some days I could see her children. With her, my illusions became reality.

We never had money, never owned anything except parts of toys—one roller skate; an old baseball given to us by our uncle Adolfo, the baseball player; an old iron hoop which Matías kept spinning, rolling on its side for miles with a little stick; a few marbles and tops. We could reenact any movie we had seen. We were the fastest guns in the west, shooting with our fingers. We had the fastest horses, that ran wild, as we made the noise of thundering hooves.

There is such beautiful innocence that comes with deprivation.

We were raised with traditions that become very meaningful as one grows older. In San Diego, the Spanish priests had brought over the European tradition of communicating with the townspeople through the church bell. The good news and the bad were passed on to us with the ringing of the bell as John Donne so eloquently said in his 1624 poem.

I remember that on Sunday mornings Father Zavala had us ring the large deep sounding bell an hour before Mass, and it broke out in repeated metallic peals that penetrated throughout the sleeping town. Every fifteen minutes he would nod and one of us—my uncles Juan or Matías, or my brother Richard and I—dressed in our starched red cassocks, wearing shoes for the first time that week, would all hold on to the large rope and tug at it with all our might, the weight of the swinging bell picking us up from the floor on the upswing.

Father Zavala himself would ring the large bell to announce the deaths in the little town and it would toll on and on, a woeful sound of death which bound the town together. He would ring the small bell for the death of a child, a higher, lighter, sadder tone announcing the unfairness of life. We would stop the game of marbles, tops, *la chusa*, or baseball to hear the sound fade away, reminded of our own mortality. My mother, Marillita, and my grandmother, María, would stop the old washing machine. The soulful peals would continue their mourning. No words needed to be spoken. We would run barefoot to the church to find Father Zavala resting against the wall, an old man exhausted from ringing the bell. He would straighten up, clear his throat, and announce the dead person's name.

Off we'd run back home, our feet burning on the asphalt under the scorching sun, reciting the name over and over to be sure we would not forget, would not announce the wrong name.

One time we did get it wrong, and my grandmother cried all afternoon for her favorite cousin until the self same cousin showed up, asking for a cup of flour. According to my grandmother, who loved to exaggerate, she clutched her heart and fell backwards into a chair. She thought she had seen a ghost she said. We had to stay away from her home for a while until she forgave us.

Regardless of who died, as far as my grandmother was concerned it was always a relative. It could be a cousin ten times removed on my grandfather's aunt's side. And she would cry, not wailing as when my grandfather died. But still she cried. And she would get my mother to start crying, both of them trying to dry the tears from their eyes with their soapy hands, feeding the wash into the rollers.

It was as my grandfather had said years before: my grandmother María should hire out for wakes and funerals to prime the mourners, to keep the wailing going.

We'd leave our marbles on the ground and run to the printer who was busy by now laying type for the *esquela*, the official death announcement. It stated the person's name, date of birth and death, relatives, and the dates and times for the rosary and for the funeral. The printer would dip the printing machine in the blackest ink he had, so that the letters would stand out against the gray background of the paper, rolling out from the press the color of death.

It was our job to distribute the *esquelas*. Holding on to the car door and standing on the running-board, we went about town, jumping off the car and running to slip a notice in the handle of every screen door. If the person was important, we got paid ten cents, a quarter.

That night Dr. Dunlap would go through town in his car with Clementina, his nurse, by his side and showing him where everyone lived who had called to complain of shortness of breath. Sometimes he had so many people to see that he wouldn't arrive at our house until well after our bedtime and he'd catch us asleep. But we would wake up just to see him. To us it was all a game, but to Dr. Dunlap it was work, and we ended up killing him from overwork when all the time we thought we were being kind to him.

When he took out his magical stethoscope, we were in awe. He didn't have to ask for silence. You could almost hear my grandmother's heartbeat as she sat straight in her large wicker chair like a queen. He would gently place the bell of the instrument on my grandmother's chest and move it around once in a while, asking questions of Clementina. Clementina translated the questions into Spanish. Had she eaten a lot of fried foods? No, sir. Never. We would laugh. Everything my grandmother ate had been cooked in lard. How long had she felt bad? Since this morning when she was kneading the dough for *tortillas* and she had heard the tolling of the bell. Finally, Dr. Dunlap would roll up the stethoscope around his hand, look my grandmother in the eye and tell her she had the heart of a young woman. What a joy it was. We could go out and play, knowing our grandmother would live to knead more dough.

I visit the cemetery in San Diego every time I go. It seems the proper thing to do, to go pay my respects to the people there I love so much: to my mother, Marillita; my father, Gonzalo; my grandmother, María and my grandfather, Gonzalo, who died suddenly coming out of the meat market, clutching his package of meat to his chest—witnesses said he was dead before he hit the ground. Next to them my uncle Juan, who became a musician, dead at thirty-three. My little sister, Belinda, died needlessly of dysentery. We baptized her with tap water because the priest could not come to the house to baptize her and give her the last rites. My uncle Mercé, insane, but generous and kind, who knew everyone's birthday and cursed everyone in town. Next to him is Adolfo, his brother, the baseball player, buried in name only since shortly after he bought his tombstone already a mindless old man was kidnapped from San Diego by someone who claimed to be his illegitimate son. He's buried in San Antonio. Then my great-grandfather, who lived to be almost one hundred years and spent a week in agony before dying while we played marbles outside his window. And my aunt Pepa, the crazy one, who lost all her children in one year.

The list goes on: García, Saenz, González, Garza, Arguijo, Flores, Everett.

The ringing of the bell never ends.

There is a universality to mankind. There are no bad towns. A little town in south Texas is the little town in John Donne's England where someone also runs to the church to ask for whom the bell tolls.

Lastly, I have discovered that regardless how great a poet John Donne was, he was not entirely right. Surely the bell tolls for everyone, but the other person's death does not diminish me. On the contrary, each one of us, by having lived, magnifies the soul of everyone else.

And now a word about these stories. All of them are a testament to the love and joy of being raised as a Mexican American in deep South Texas. There is no other place like it in the world and I feel privileged to have been born and raised there. If fiction is the enhancement of reality through illusion, like for Pepa, then these stories are fiction. If you believe reality can be an illusion, like for Mercé, then these stories are true. Rest assured that none of them happened exactly as I have written. On the other hand, all that I have written is true.

Confession

We were raised to believe that confession was the one sacrament of the Catholic Church which afforded us all an everlasting life in Heaven. "If," my grandmother used to say, "Father Zavala pardons your sins."

Father Zavala was no problem, despite the warning from my grandmother. He dispensed pardons and penance to everyone. We knew that as long as Father Zavala was alive we had nothing to worry about. No matter what sinful things we did, what horrible thoughts we had, Father Zavala would ask God to give him the power to forgive us, and we were absolutely positive God gave him the power.

So we were sure to follow my mother's and grandmother's admonishments, and every Friday night we would go to confession. In fact, we would arrive early so we could play at the park across the street while the drone of the praying of the Rosary could be heard. We wrestled with each other, getting the itchy grass under our clothes while someone watched out for the priest, keeping an eye on the church and the rectory.

Soon the old women dressed in black looking like crows after a heavy meal, emerged having finished the Rosary. They would linger outside, talk about the day—how things had been, who had died, who was sick, and who had a sick or a dead relative. For death was their common bond.

Their duties done, satisfied the daily vital information of the little town had been passed around, they would disperse in all directions by ones and two and threes and fours, my grandmother among them. She could not see us across the street. We would giggle behind the bushes to hear her talk so animatedly to the other women, as though it was a surprise to us and not the usual way in which she behaved. It was just that hearing her and seeing her from afar seemed to exaggerate her mannerisms.

After Rosary, at seven in the evening, Father Zavala would come out of the screened porch at the rear of the rectory in a great hurry, ready to hear confessions. We would watch him spring down the stairs and stride on the sidewalk under the grape vinery which connected the church to the rectory. As soon as he closed the church door, we would run and meet him inside the church halfway down the center aisle. He would greet us by squeezing our ears between his fat fingers. It was impossible to get away from him, as stout as he was. He could stretch out his arms, herd us against the pews, and have us surrounded by his flesh. One or two at a time, he would subject us to this ear-wrenching torture. We allowed him this pleasure at our expense because my grandmother always reminded us that we were not to make Father Zavala angry if we wanted to go to Heaven.

We knew that he liked us for we brought him some laughter in the drudging solitude that was his daily life.

Father Zavala had worn thin the gold band on his finger, twirling it while he prayed. He wore a small wooden cross around his neck which his mother had sent him. He bathed infrequently. My grandmother said priests had no one to smell good for. The dandruff from his eyebrows floated occasionally from his brow like a white mold shaken off a dead limb. No matter his age, to us he was always old. He had come to town old and had remained old and gray-headed.

Despite his loneliness, Father Zavala acquired and maintained a good sense of humor as well as a ruddy complexion the wine he drank reinforced. He hurried everywhere he went. Administering the last rites was for him a race against time—lighting candles sloppily, rushing about the dying, trying to do everything at one time. Still, when he spoke inside the church, it was without feeling. His Masses, Rosaries, Stations of the Cross, everything, were all in a lifeless monotone that let us know how tired he had become with the repetitive nature of his work. We often wondered how he could maintain his sanity living in the sameness of each day. Not that he didn't love being a priest. Many times he would tell us that the love for God, Jesus and the Holy Ghost was the ultimate love in the world. Privately, we could not believe this. To us, to love a ghost was not possible. We had seen the

ghosts dancing on the wall at night by lantern light at my
uncle Mercé's house and had been so scared of them we could
not sleep.

Away from the church, a man freed of his trappings,
Father Zavala took on a different air. His eyes danced when
he spoke. He joked and laughed with the people.

Usually, we had no major sins to confess. So we would sit
on the grass, in between our wrestling, trying to figure out
what stories we could make up to tell Father Zavala in the
confessional.

Once inside the church, we would stand as close to the
confessional as he allowed, listening to other people's woes
and poking each other in the ribs. Then Father Zavala in the
almost empty and darkened church, would clear his throat, a
sound so resonant and menacing that it quieted us immediately.

On this night, with the church windows open, we could
hear the sounds of the locusts coming from the creek. A dog
barked just long enough to irritate the neighbors. We waited
for the dog to resume his barking. A firefly floated in through
the window, flew around the lighted votive candles, and then
went to settle on the shoulder of one of the saints. It crawled
around the saint's beard, flickering its little tail light off and
on. Being a Catholic, I tried to attach some divine importance
to this random act. What could God possibly be telling us?
That the church was about to catch on fire? That we ought to
deposit ten cents and light a candle in a saint's name? Were
we going to receive money? This would be my grandmother's
favorite interpretation.

Cota pinched me and told me to pay attention to what the
old lady in the confessional was saying. She was having trouble with her husband. He drank too much and worked too little, a familiar lament. To add insult to the injuries suffered
by the wife, the man had another woman on the side. How
could he afford her, Father Zavala asked. But the woman, to
the amazed satisfaction of the priest could not come up with
an answer.

The woman came out, saw us standing close enough to
have heard her confession. She recognized us and we recognized her. She was one of the many ladies who liked to visit
my grandmother, one of the many who my grandmother
would hide from when she saw her coming toward the house.

She gave us a disgusted look, threw her head up in the air, and rushed straight to the altar rail. Cota followed her and watched her cross herself several times and begin to pray, beating her chest gently.

My aunt Maggie went first, and we heard her confess to killing a wren at the creek. What a surprise that was to us all! We had planned to confess to having had bad thoughts. Father Zavala, very serious, asked her how the death had occurred. Maggie had not expected Father Zavala to be so interested in the death of a little bird. Usually she was the first to go in, would come out very fast, pray one or two Hail Marys, one or two Our Fathers, an Act of Contrition, and that would be it. Tonight, Father Zavala wanted to know how the bird had died.

Maggie stammered and delayed, lied some more, piled lies upon lies, and finally began to cry. Feeling trapped by her own lies, she decided to blame someone else. She confessed she had not killed the bird. She confessed she had lied. Her brother, Juan, she cried to the priest, had killed the bird.

Father Zavala peeked out through the curtain that enclosed the entrance to the confessional, and motioned for Juan to step in. He excused Maggie. Maggie came out and Juan stepped in. Father Zavala wanted Juan to explain the death of the wren. Juan began his story, making it long, adding dialog—all lies. Finally, he explained to the priest in the greatest detail how, when he had the little bird in his sights and was about to shoot it with the sling-shot, his brother Matías had become overly excited and had shot the bird instead. The bird crawled out from its nest, tried to fly, flapped its wings, and teetered on the limb. It lost its grip on the limb and clung to it with one foot, hanging upside down. Then the bird let out a terrible shriek to alert her little babies in the nest to the fact that she had been mortally wounded. Not until that moment did the bird lose its grip, spiral down like a kite without a tail, and fall, making a horrible sound as it hit against a rock by the creek. Juan told Father Zavala the wren had a hole on the side of its face where Matías had shot it. There was blood all over. By now, Father Zavala was both confused and angry. He cleared his throat again, this time heavily, a sign of irritation. We heard him ask God if there was anyone in our family who ever told the truth?

Juan came out of the confessional with a load of prayers to offer throughout the church. He winked at Matías as Father Zavala angrily asked for Matías to step in. Matías was not more than three feet away.

Matías went in, knelt down, and began to tell Father Zavala his version of the lie. He claimed he had not killed the wren intentionally. He was trying to scare away a hawk that was trying to kill the wren and her babies. He was not good with the sling-shot, he explained to the old man. He had aimed for the hawk and killed the wren instead. He felt so horrible about it he had not been able to sleep. He was having nightmares over the episode. We heard Father Zavala give out a soft whistle of concern. Matías continued his lament. He had misfired while trying to do a good deed. Furthermore, Matías told the priest very seriously, that that was what he got for trying to be good. This triggered a fit of rage. Father Zavala yanked open the curtain to the confessional almost tearing it off its rings, reached across the perforated sheet metal that separated him from Matías, and grabbed Matías by his thick hair. He escorted Matías to the center aisle and told him to go pray. He sentenced him to four Hail Marys, four Our Fathers and four Acts of Contrition for killing the bird and four more of each for adding lies to the story. Matías complained to Father Zavala that he had lied a lot less than his brother Juan. Father Zavala then told him to be quiet and to go pray. Father Zavala then looked around for Juan to add some more prayers to his penance, but Juan and Maggie had left, having said only a few of their assigned prayers. They were at the park smoking a cigarette while waiting for us.

My aunt Cota was walking through the pews looking for coins which might have fallen out the pockets of the women at the Rosary earlier. When Father Zavala called her in, she knew nothing of what had been said. She had been too far away from the confessional to hear the lie Maggie had started. Father Zavala asked her who had killed the bird. Cota was stunned. She was prepared to confess to bad thoughts. She was very resourceful though, a great liar, and an expert at theatrics. She regained her composure very quickly. She had not heard of the bird, but she knew the others well enough to realize that she needed to come up with something bold. She confessed she had killed the bird, whatever bird it might be. She confessed she killed birds all the time—all sizes, colors, and shapes—using rocks, slingshots, guns. She killed horned toads all the time, too, she said. She had made horned toads smoke cigarettes before she killed them. Father Zavala let out a sigh which filled the church. He got after her very sternly. He had never known this side of her. She had always appeared to be a pleasant young girl. Did she not know it was a sin to kill God's creatures?

Frances then said out loud that we had seen Father Zavala's yardman kill a goat in the churchyard between the rectory and the church. We all said we had seen him slit its throat. We were grumbling. Father Zavala stuck his head out again and put his finger up to his mouth to ask for quiet. He informed us that the killing of an animal for food was perfectly appropriate in God's eyes.

From the altar where he was saying his basketful of Hail Marys, Our Fathers and Acts of Contritions, Matías stood up and said we had eaten the wren. It had been our food just as the goat had been the priest's food.

We all agreed to that. It was true. One time when we had killed a wren, we had pulled the feathers and roasted the wren on an open fire like we had seen the cowboys do in the movies.

Father Zavala proclaimed our innocence then. We had not sinned. He seemed relieved to get that out of the way.

He pointed at my sister Sylvia and she went into the confessional. We crept up close in order to listen. For some reason, Maggie had started out the evening with a lie and everyone seemed unable to confess to bad thoughts. Sylvia confessed to being disrespectful to our grandmother. Father Zavala wanted to know what she had said, and Sylvia made something up quickly, saying she had told our grandmother she was a witch. When we heard Sylvia say "witch" we started to giggle. That was a new one on us. Father Zavala got after her enough to make the confession worthwhile. Her penance was two Our Fathers and two Acts of Contrition and a promise from Sylvia that she would never again call our grandmother a witch. Later, Sylvia said to our grandmother that she could call her a witch one time without having to go to confession. She had already done penance ahead of time. It was like having money in the bank.

My brother Richard confessed to saying bad words, and there Father Zavala drew the line. He didn't want to hear what my brother had said. He had made the mistake with Matías one time, and Matías had been glad to repeat the bad words. My brother received, for punishment, one Our Father and one Act of Contrition.

At that age, Frances was the timid one in the family, and trying to get her to make up a sin to confess was hard. Tonight she was stubborn. She knelt inside the darkness of the confessional while Father Zavala tried to get her to confess to something, anything. He asked her questions upon questions and Frances kept answering "No." Then, when Father Zavala could go no further, Frances blurted out that she had once seen a man and a woman kissing in the belfry at the back of the church.

Father Zavala asked who the couple was. Could Frances identify the couple? Frances said no. It was too dark and she had run as soon as she saw the couple. Had they been doing anything besides kissing? Frances wouldn't know. She had seen them kissing, an old man and a woman. Father Zavala remained quiet for a time, not knowing whether to believe this story or not. He proclaimed Frances to be free of sin. She had inadvertently seen something she should not have. In the future, if she saw the couple again she was to try to identify them and contact him immediately. Father Zavala stuck his head out and informed us all that it was our responsibility to watch out for this couple so that he could punish them. Finally, the priest gave Frances one Our Father and an Act of Contrition in case she had forgotten some vague sin in her past which she had never confessed.

Since no one else had confessed to bad thoughts, I figured it was up to me. I confessed to having bad thoughts, and when Father Zavala asked me what those thoughts were, I didn't know what to say. Cota leaned in and whispered into my ear. I repeated what Cota had told me. I had thought of a naked girl. Father Zavala admonished me about such thoughts, thoughts which he said led to corruption and degradation of the human spirit. I should be chaste. I agreed and accepted the harshest sentence so far that Friday night: ten Our Father's, ten Hail Mary's, ten Acts of Contrition, and the Stations of the Cross—all for being what he called a degenerate, whatever that meant.

I could hear the rest of my family playing in the park while I was inside saying my penance under the watchful eye of Father Zavala as he shut down the church for the night.

Later on, after the church was locked, he would sit on one of the concrete benches at the park and smoke his cigarettes. We would join him, sitting around him while he told us stories about Spain.

For some demented reason, he loved to distract us by pointing at a star. And while our gaze was turned upward, he would try to burn us with his cigarette. He never could, though. We were much too cagey and fast for the old man.

Baseball

We loved to play baseball. We would take the old mesquite stick and the old ball across the street to the parochial school grounds to play a game. Father Zavala enjoyed watching us. We could hear him laugh mightily from the screened porch at the rear of the rectory where he sat smoking his cigarettes.

The way we played baseball was to rotate positions after every out. First base, the only base we used, was located where one would normally find second base. This made the batter have to run past the pitcher and a long way to first baseman, increasing the odds of getting thrown out. The pitcher stood in line with the batter, and with first base, and could stand as close or as far from the batter as he or she wanted. Aside from the pitcher, the batter and the first baseman, we had a catcher. All the rest of us would stand in the outfield. After an out, the catcher would come up to bat. The pitcher took the position of catcher, and the first baseman moved up to be the pitcher. Those in the outfield were left to their own devices. I don't remember ever getting to bat.

There was one exception to the rotation scheme. I don't know who thought of this, but whoever caught the ball on the fly would go directly to be the batter. This was not a popular thing to do. You could expect to have the ball thrown at you on the next pitch.

There was no set distance for first base. First base was wherever Matías or Juan or Cota tossed a stone. They were the law. The distance could be long or short depending on how soon we thought we were going to be called in to eat. The size of the stone marking the base mattered more than the distance from home plate to first base. If we hadn't been called in to eat by dusk, first base was hard to find. Sometimes someone would kick the stone farther away and arguments erupted.

When the batter hit the ball in the air and it was caught that was an out. So far so good. But if the ball hit the ground, the fielder had two choices. One, in keeping with the standard rules of the game, the ball could be thrown to the first baseman and, if caught before the batter arrived to the base, that was an out. But the second, more interesting option allowed the fielder, ball in hand, to take off running after the batter. When close enough, the fielder would throw the ball at the batter. If the batter was hit before reaching first base, the batter was out. But if the batter evaded being hit with the ball, he or she could, run to first base, run back to home plate. All the while, everyone was chasing the batter, picking up the ball and throwing it at him or her. To complicate matters, on the way to home plate the batter had the choice of running anywhere possible to avoid getting hit. For example, the batter could run to hide behind the hackberry trees at the parochial school grounds, going from tree to tree until he or she could make it safely back to home plate. Many a time we would wind up playing the game past Father Zavala and in front of the rectory half a block away. Or we could be seen running after the batter several blocks down the street toward town, trying to hit the batter with the ball. One time we wound up all the way across town before we cornered Juan against a fence, hold him down, and hit him with the ball. Afterwards, we all fell laughing in a pile on top of each other, exhausted from the run through town.

The old codgers, the old shiftless men who spent their day talking at the street corners, never caught on to what we were doing. They would halt their idle conversation just long enough to watch us run by them, hollering and throwing the old ball at the batter.

It was the only kind of baseball game Father Zavala had ever seen. What a wonderful game it must have been for him to see us hit the ball, run to a rock, then run for our lives down the street. He loved the game, shouting from the screened porch at us, pushing us on. And then all of a sudden we were gone, running after the batter. What a game! In what enormous stadium would it be played to allow such freedom over such an expanse of ground.

My uncle Adolfo, who had pitched for the Yankees and the Cardinals in the majors, had given us the ball several years before. Once when he returned for a visit, he saw us playing from across the street and walked over to ask us what we were doing.

"Playing baseball," we answered as though we thought he should know better. After all, he was the professional baseball player.

He walked away shaking his head. "What a waste of a good ball," we heard him say, marvelling at our ignorance.

Matías

Some people are born to curse and some are not. The ones who find cursing awkward lack certain personality. If they do curse, it comes off as vulgar. They raise eyebrows instead of laughter. The ones who are born to curse can get by with it. It becomes them, and once their reputation is established, it is just as much a part of their makeup as the smile on their faces. Matías was one of those. All the rest of us hardly ever cursed. But Matías cursed for all of us. And he was original. Matías would create curse words. Where one would use a simple curse word, Matías would add to it, give it a new beginning, starting the curse with four or five words of introduction, going into the curse word itself and then finishing it off with four, five, and sometimes six other inventive words. It was like listening to a short story. There was a beginning, a middle, and an end. We all thought it was something to admire.

My grandfather considered Matías very creative. He would laugh at the things Matías would come up with. Only when company was present did he mockingly object if Matías cursed.

"Hush," he would say. "Don't you know we have company?" And that would be the extent of it.

It was not that Matías tried very hard at it either. The words just seemed to flow out of his mouth like honey from a jar, an effortless thing, something of a *don* or God-given gift.

One day we had gone with the old mesquite stick and the old ball to play our own strange brand of baseball at the parochial school ground. Matías' time to bat came. Maggie was catching. Juan was pitching. Cota was the first baseman. All the rest of us were in the outfield. Juan wound up to throw like he had seen our Uncle Adolfo do. But he closed his eyes when he threw the ball. The ball headed straight for Matías who thought Juan was teasing him and was throwing a curve. Juan had bragged to our Uncle Adolfo that he could throw a curve, but he couldn't. When Matías finally realized the ball was on its way to hit him, he turned his back and that's where he got hit. Matías turned red with anger. Juan said Matías was out since the ball had hit him. Matías began his extended curse in a loud voice. He cursed Juan, starting from the moment of his conception to his passage through the fallopian tubes to his arrival into his mother's womb, his birth, his present and future life.

Father Zavala had been sitting at the rectory in the screened porch enjoying us play, smoking his cigarettes. He had been admiring the love and cooperation we showed each other. What a beautiful set of children we were. Not having children, he always fell into the trap of great expectations. Presently, when he heard all the cursing of which Matías was capable, he got up and went inside. He had heard Matías curse before, but this day, we all agreed, Matías had graduated into another class.

That same night, after the Rosary, Father Zavala rushed out of the sacristy, ran through the yard, and waited in the garage in hopes of intercepting my mother and grandmother. He lit his cigarette and was smoking pleasantly when the two women, in a group with three others, walked past the garage on their way home. He stepped out, first clearing his throat so as not to frighten them. He called out my grandmother and my mother. They approached him while the other women said their goodbyes and continued on their way. As he walked along with them, Father Zavala informed them what had happened earlier in the day. Matías' tongue had to be curbed.

"I'm afraid the poor child will never go to heaven as he is," Father Zavala estimated.

"Well, we can't have that," said my grandmother. "All my family has gone to heaven."

Father Zavala declined a cup of coffee and stopped at the corner by the house. From there he said his farewell and returned to the rectory.

As always, the next morning my grandfather left town for work, and it was up to my grandmother to cure Matías of this nasty habit.

We all volunteered plans, all involving physical punishment. We wanted to see Matías whipped outside in the yard. My grandmother would have none of that. If we would leave her alone, she would come up with a plan, she said.

She went into her room, took out her Rosary, and began to pray for guidance. We were playing outside her room and we could hear the murmurings of the Rosary. My mother interrupted her to give her iced tea and food. My grandmother kept on. At around ten at night she came out of her room looking tired and careworn. Her hair was in a mess. She made no attempt to keep it off her forehead. The black skirt she was wearing was twisted off center, the front button to one side. Her blouse had stains on it as if she had gone through a crying spell. She sat at the kitchen table and asked for a cup of coffee which my mother was pleased to give her. She sipped quietly as we sat around her, Matías, the culprit, included. He was as anxious as anyone else to know what fruitful resolution her day of agony had brought her.

My grandmother had decided, she informed us, to fall back on the remedies of Don Pedrito Jaramillo, the great South Texas faith-healer long dead long before. My grandmother had assisted Don Pedrito as a young woman, and had a lot of faith in his herbal treatments. She believed that herbs, either rubbed into the skin of the affected area or used to make baths or washes to soak the body, would heal ailments.

We kept quiet as she sat at the table drinking her coffee, contemplating what particular herb Don Pedrito would have used to cure Matías of his cursing. By the time she finished her second cup of coffee, she came up with the solution.

"This is what he would have used," she said, speaking reverently of the faith-healer. She asked for a pencil and paper and wrote the letter T on the paper.

It was to be *toronjil*, the most bitter herb imaginable. She made a tea out of it, and every night before bedtime she fed it to Matías. Matías took it like the strong person he was, without a word of complaint. When that didn't work, she had him soak in it nightly. Still the cursing continued.

By now she had forgotten about the Rosary and her prayer. She consulted with the spirit of Don Pedrito, imploring his guidance. She thought one night she had heard the dead man speak to her of pomegranates. Immediately she went out into the yard and dug up the pomegranate root, what was left of it after an episode with my stuttering. She boiled it and fed it to Matías. That didn't work either. She drenched him in pomegranate solutions as I had been. The cursing was worse after a week, and we were all laughing at her efforts.

Finally, when she was running out of herbs, she called on Father Zavala.

"For all purposes," she explained to the priest, "I have dug up most of the yard looking for herbs, roots and leaves to feed to the boy or soak him in. Nothing seems to work."

Father Zavala was patient with her, not showing his displeasure because she had shown more faith in Don Pedrito than in prayer. Long ago he had realized that the religious mentality of the Mexican-American always incorporated an element of witchcraft. When he first arrived from Spain, he had tried to abolish this form of worship, but he quickly realized that to do so alienated him from the people. He couldn't change them, so he ignored this practice.

"When I was a young boy," Father Zavala said, "I would stutter, much to my father's consternation. My own mother, just like you, María, went to the town priest for advice."

"And what advice did he give your sanctified mother?" my grandmother asked.

"He recommended something very, very common in Spain at the time—scaring the child when he least expects it. The shock from such a scare seemed to help. My own mother tried it on me. She stole into my room one night while I slept, and she screamed into my ear. I shot out of bed, running around the room. I saw my dear mother bracing herself against my bed. Confused, I ran to her arms and repeated her name over and over again without a stutter. She knelt down, and we both prayed. It was something of a miracle. My father was happy. I could speak normally from then on."

"And you preach such beautiful sermons," my grandmother complimented him. "Sometimes you make me cry. One would never guess that you had trouble speaking at one time."

That was enough for my grandmother. She formulated her plan on the way back from the rectory. If she was to scare Matías, it would have to be her secret and hers alone. No one would know what she was to do or when. She went around during the day humming, acting smug. She had found her answer. When we tried to pry out of her what Father Zavala had said, she would only smile.

"I should have known," she contemplated, looking out the window into the street while washing dishes, "that Father Zavala would help me."

She had given up on Don Pedrito, the faith-healer. She was back to her Rosary. She prayed quietly into the night, staying awake to hear any noise coming from the boy's room.

Her patience paid off. In the middle of the night, after a few days, she heard a door knob move. She put her Rosary down. The door knob made its familiar squeaking sound. My grandmother got up as light as a mouse. She went to her door, opened it slightly, and peered out into the hall. The door to the boy's room was opening. Soon a barefooted Matías wearing only his pants came out into the hall, yawned and stretched. Half asleep, he drifted aimlessly toward the rear door. My grandmother was about to scream at him when she decided he was too far off. He was at the back door by then. Matías stepped out. My grandmother tip-toed behind him and stood at the door, watching Matías go off into the dark night. He was on his way to the outdoor toilet. Quickly, she went out without a sound and followed Matías. Matías stopped as though he had heard her footsteps. He looked around. A dog howled in the distance, setting off other dogs in the neighborhood. My grandmother froze. Matías could not see her, his eyes full of sleep. He yawned, rubbed his eyes, and continued on his way. He went into the toilet and closed the door. My grandmother ran behind the toilet and peeked in through a crack between the boards to see Matías in the moonlight, sitting at one of the two holes. She could hear him talking to himself, cursing about something. Here was her opportunity. She inhaled a huge ball of air which filled her lungs to bursting. She forced out the air all at once, creating the most horrible scream anyone had ever heard. Her own voice startled even her and made the hair on the back of her neck stand on end.

Matías was so surprised, so taken aback by the scream, that he jumped off the hole and fell to the floor. His pants were tangled around his feet. He tried frantically to pull his pants up. By now he had begun the introduction for his curse word. He ran around inside the small outdoor toilet, bouncing off the walls, struggling with his pants, kicking at the door. The main body of the curse was gushing from his mouth. As he continued to struggle with his pants, he ended the curse in a loud scream, the worst curse word in the Spanish language—the one about the mother—and dedicated it to "whoever screamed at me!"

He had cursed his own mother.

My grandmother dutifully reported her experience to Father Zavala. He did not want her to repeat the words.

"He started the curse," my grandmother said anyway, "almost from the beginning of time, and it grew more and more until he ended cursing his sanctified mother."

"Ave María purísima!" cried Father Zavala. He scratched his head with his crucifix and said, "We must think of something else."

It seemed Father Zavala had more remedies than there were curse words. We soaked Matías in pine oil and had him take mesquite bean baths. We covered him with cow dung, horse dung, goat dung and rubbed chicken droppings over him. We made him drink epsom salt, pomegranate tea, and calf urine. We flogged him with horse hair, lit candles around his bed at night, and when that didn't work, placed a raw egg under his bed to see if he had been possessed. Nothing worked. Matías' cursing continued.

In the end, Father Zavala decided not to count this sin against him in the confessional. As far as we know, Matías was the only person the Church had ever granted license to curse.

"It is not a sin, María," Father Zavala explained to my grandmother. She was worried Matías could never get to Heaven. "It's more of a misuse of language. Let us leave the boy alone to see if he will outgrow this horrible tendency."

To his everlasting credit, he never did. He would not have been Matías otherwise.

Tío Nano

My grandmother's house was always filled with *tíos*—uncles—the few who were there for a cup of coffee and a visit, the many who were there for a meal.

Their expressions of surprise when my grandmother finally put a plate of food in front of one of them always amused us. "Oh, no," they would protest, waving hands in front of their faces, "I can't eat this. I'm taking food from the children...from you, María."

"No...no...no," my grandmother would say, "eat it. There's plenty more left."

"Are you sure?"

"Yes. Eat."

Then as they ate hurriedly, they would stop long enough to say, "This is the best I have ever eaten. You are the best, María. I told the men who hang around the streets just yesterday that you were the best cook in the world. 'She can take,' I said, 'one pound of hamburger meat and make *picadillo* and feed twenty people.' That's what I said. 'And if you add beans...well, no telling how many more. A whole troop of men. She ought to open up a restaurant.'"

"Do you want more?" my grandmother would ask, extending her hand toward the plate.

"A little, if you don't mind," they would reply, hoping not to have offended my grandmother by wiping their mouths with their sleeves and picking up the plate and handing it to her. "Just enough to finish this little bit of tortilla," they would comment as an excuse, looking at us sitting around the table watching them eat.

"Another tortilla?" she would ask the *tío*.

"Well..well, no. Well...just one to finish the meal. What can one do? One has to have one to finish the meal."

Hernando Carrejo, *Tío* Nano we called him, was a master at timing his visits at mealtime. We could see him coming from the highway by the courthouse two blocks away, stooped from the weight of two suitcases full of clothes to be sold to the people living in the south Texas ranches. From his home in Laredo, he would take the bus or hitch a ride that would get him past Freer and around the ranching community of La Rosita. From there he would work his way through the ranches showing off his wares. In a few days, hungry and tired, he would find his way back to the main road and hitch a ride to San Diego to see his favorite cousin, my grandmother.

Then came the depression, and my grandmother grew tired of feeding and housing so many people, especially *Tío* Nano, who ate enough for two men, and we were told to be on the lookout for him. Anyone seeing *Tío* Nano coming down the road was to alert my grandmother, giving her time to hide not only the food she was cooking, but herself. We were supposed to tell him she was not home, that she had left town.

We were playing out in the street close to the courthouse one late morning when an old black car coming from the direction of Freer stopped at the corner. We heard *Tío* Nano's distinctive slurred voice thanking the driver for the ride and we saw him climb out of the car, shiny rear-end first, having a difficult time getting his suitcases out from the back seat. We dropped everything and ran home before he could turn around to see us.

My grandmother was in the kitchen when we arrived.

"What in Heaven's name happened to you?" she asked.

"*Tío* Nano," Cota managed to spit out before going to the faucet to get a drink of water.

"He's here?" my grandmother inquired, her face ashen, looking at all of us one at a time.

"Yes," we said.

"God in Heaven," she cried out. "I have to hide the food."

She grabbed for two dirty hand towels to grasp the pot of boiling beans and rushed with it into the bathroom. She came running out of the bathroom and snatched the plate of tortillas and raced with it to the bathroom where she had just hidden the beans. As she was running back out, she said, "Tell him I'm gone. Tell him I left. Went to Alice to buy groceries, and I won't return until...Well, not today. That won't work. Tell him I got sick and had to go see Dr. Dunlap. I'll be at the doctor's until midnight. No. He'll wait up for me. Tell him I went somewhere...anywhere. Make up a lie."

She ran into the bathroom and locked herself in. From inside we heard her muffled voice. "Tell him whatever you want. Make something up. Get rid of him."

We went outside to sit on the porch and wait for the man struggling with his suitcases. I would be sent out to peek into the street to see where he was in his journey. I in turn would shout out his position. Finally, I ran to the porch as he entered the yard. He greeted us all and let out a big sigh.

"How is María, my favorite cousin?" he asked.

"She is fine," Juan replied.

"But she's not here," Maggie said.

"Where did she go?" *Tío* Nano asked.

"We don't know. She just took off," Cota replied, trying to divert his attention by picking up a marble with her toes.

The news stunned him. He had come all this way and would not get a meal. He dropped his suitcases like heavy leaden weights and rubbed his arms. He climbed the porch steps and went to look into the kitchen through the screen door.

"It smells like beans," he said to himself.

"Cota is making beans," Frances informed him.

Satisfied that no one was in the kitchen, he came back to sit on the porch steps between his suitcases. He took an old handkerchief out of his rear pocket and wiped his brow. He let out a moan so full of disappointment that it almost made us ill. He had missed a meal.

"Like she took off? And no one knows where she went?" he asked desperately. He refolded his handkerchief. "Just gone?" he continued, furrowing his brow into a question.

"Yes," we replied. "Just gone."

"And no one went after her?"

"No," we replied.

"We couldn't," Juan explained. "If we had tried, she would have killed us."

"Killed you?" Nano asked.

"Yes, killed us," Matías replied.

"She's gone crazy before," Cota broke the news to him.

He skewered up his face. He was having trouble absorbing such a bizarre account.

"We caught her eating soap," Frances said, and we began to laugh.

"That is nothing to be laughing about," *Tío* Nano scolded us. "I find it hard to believe that María, as strong as she is, has gone crazy and left. And you don't know where she went?"

"No, we don't," said Matías. "But she screamed, saying she would write when she got there."

"It couldn't be far," Cota said. "She was on foot, running to the creek when we saw her the last time."

"Heaven help her," *Tío* Nano said. He scratched his forehead softly with his short fingers, contemplating the fate which had taken his favorite cousin from him. "And the authorities? What do they say?"

"They're looking for her right now," Maggie said.

"The whole town is looking for her," Juan added.

Tío Nano looked toward our house across the way and asked, "And Marillita, the children's mother? Is she home?"

"No," we all answered.

"She's out looking for her, too," said Matías.

Tío Nano finally asked, "Well, exactly what happened?"

Cota stood up to better embellish the story. She said, "Let me tell you, *Tío* Nano. She was cooking. She was at the stove. Cooking. It was very hot. *Tío* Juanito was here eating for free like he always does. María was at the stove turning her tortillas, flipping them over to *Tío* Juanito. *Tío* Juanito was eating like a machine. Suddenly, she let out a scream like she had burned herself."

"And then," Matías stood up to continue, "she came at *Tío* Juanito with a knife in her hand. She came slowly at him. Her face had changed. She looked like a monster. She raised the knife over her head and tried to kill him. She swung the knife and hit the table. We were screaming. We all ran out of the kitchen and stood on the porch, shaking like leaves. We could hear *Tío* Juanito begging for his life. My mother was screaming at him. If he ate another tortilla, she yelled, she was going to kill him."

"Then," Juan stood up to say, "*Tío* Juanito came out running with a piece of tortilla stuck in his mouth. He was trying to say something, but he couldn't. We saw him run off and we haven't seen him since."

"He left one boot behind," Maggie said.

"And then María ran off?" *Tío* Nano asked us.

"Yes," Cota said. "She came out running after *Tío* Juanito."

"She had the knife in her teeth," Frances said.

"How awful," said *Tío* Nano.

Matías said, "Juanito took off toward the courthouse, and María took off toward the creek."

"What a strange turn this has been," *Tío* Nano said, looking off into space. "If you would have asked me what was the least likely thing to happen to María, it would have been that she would lose her mind. But," he continued, "you children come from a family with mental problems. You have Mercé and Pepa, both insane. María now. What a shame."

He checked his handkerchief and shook his head. He placed the handkerchief back in his rear pocket. "Now that I think about it, I should have known," he said slowly, thinking about my grandmother and where she could have gone to. "I should have known it would happen. Poor María. It's the world we live in. The Depression has got to her. The Republicans. Hoover. Gonzalo gone to San Antonio to find a job. All her children at home."

"And there's no food," I informed him, that being the only thought which had come to my mind.

He took off his gray fedora, inspected the inside and ran his fingers around the leather band. He scratched his head once more and looked toward the road that would take him back to his family in Laredo. "It's that way all over the ranches," he said, and stood up and dusted his old suit with his hat. "Look at me," he demanded. "When have you ever seen me look like this? As dirty as this? I sometimes feel like going crazy, too. Like María. Let me tell you children that I don't blame María for going insane."

"I don't know," Juan said, "but we don't have any food."

He cocked an eye at Juan and said, very sternly, "I know...you children have made that quite clear. No food."

We looked up to him to see his face, and we noticed beyond him, through the screen door, a movement inside the kitchen. At first we thought we could see the shadow of another uncle who was staying with us, but then as the figure came into focus we realized who it was and our eyes widened and our mouths flew open. *Tío* Nano stared at us and must have been taken aback because he said, "Children, you look like you've seen a ghost."

We had. It was my grandmother, standing at the kitchen door. She had betrayed us once more. "Who is it?" she asked, in her most innocent voice.

Tío Nano turned around and stood quickly. He rushed to the door saying, "My God, woman. I thought that you had gone. María...the children here..."

"Nano!" she cried out in a great show of emotion as she threw open the kitchen door and stepped out to embrace him. "Blessed are these eyes that see you."

In his confusion, *Tío* Nano began to mumble in his slurred voice, "Insane. I thought you were insane." He pointed at us and said, "Gone? Gone? You children said she was gone? The knife. Killing Juanito."

"We don't have any food," Cota said, trying in the confusion of the moment to preserve at least a part of the lie.

He looked into my grandmother's eyes and with tears oozing down his face said, "María, where have you been? To the dirty creek? Hiding. Insane."

"Insane? Been?" my grandmother answered as she squeezed him, laughing. "Been? Nowhere. I was in the bathroom."

"The children..." *Tío* Nano mumbled, pointing a finger at us, "What...Why?"

My grandmother looked at us and said, still laughing, "Don't pay any attention to them. They take after their *Tío* Pacho...lying about everything. The trouble I have with them all. I just hope they outgrow it."

Tío Nano grabbed his chest with both hands, feeling for his ailing heart. "Lying is a horrible trait to have," he cried to us, trying to catch his breath. "You'll never be a man or a woman of any substance. Here you had me believing you..."

"Forget about them," my grandmother said to him, escorting him into the kitchen. "I'll take care of them after you eat."

He ate so much it almost made us sick just to watch.

Late the next morning, after a heavy breakfast of *chorizo*, eggs and tortillas, we watched as *Tío* Nano hugged my grandmother goodbye and gathered his suitcases and walked out. We waved goodbye to him as his short body swayed from side to side with the burden of his suitcases, his hat over to one side. We followed him at a distance until he got to the road. He set his suitcases down and began to hitchhike. He was there for almost the whole day before someone stopped and gave him a ride.

"I live in Laredo," we heard him say while piling his suitcases into the rear seat.

Shortly afterward, I began to stutter very badly and the others were making fun of me. So my mother and my grandmother decided to take me to the famous faith-healer in Laredo, Doña María China. "And if it gets late," my grandmother reasoned, "we'll spend the night at Nano's...God knows he owes us a lot of hospitality."

My father drove all eleven of us to Laredo early one Saturday morning. We hardly fit in the car. Doña María China examined me, asked me several questions, and decided I should be bathed nightly in pomegranate extract.

The sun was setting as she finished explaining the treatments to my mother, grandmother and father while Cota, Juan, Matías, Maggie, Frances, Sylvia, and Richard snickered in the background. By the time we got out, it was dark and both my mother and grandmother decided we would stay with *Tío* Nano at the old house on Washington Street, eat there that night, get up early the next day, eat *chorizo* with eggs and tortillas, sort of pay him back good, and then drive home.

We arrived at his house to find the door unlocked but no one there. We walked through the house, and when we got to the kitchen we found a large stack of tortillas, a huge skillet full of hamburger meat with vermicelli, and a huge skillet of refried beans. All eleven of us sat and ate with a vengeance until we could no longer eat another bite. We waited for *Tío* Nano and Lina, his wife, for the longest time. At ten o'clock, when no one had showed up, we decided to stay the night and went to bed. Around midnight my mother got us up and said she wasn't comfortable sleeping there without *Tío* Nano and Lina. My grandmother wanted to stay to make Lina cook *chorizo* with eggs and tortillas in the morning. My mother insisted, so we got dressed, got in the car, and drove back to San Diego, arriving at about three in the morning.

Doña María China must have known we had pomegranates. My father dug up, day by day after work, the old pomegranate fence my grandmother had planted years ago. My mother took the roots, washed them outside with the hose and boiled them, and then soaked me in the tub in the warm solution, using a tin cup to pour the solution over my head. Her warm smooth hand stroked my hair, forcing the bitter amber liquid down my body.

Not two months later, *Tío* Nano arrived with his suitcases full, not having sold a single item. We had to treat him royally. After all, we had eaten his food and slept in his beds. My mother was so excited to tell him about our stay at his house and about how wonderful the tortillas, the hamburger with vermicelli, and the refried beans had been.

Tío Nano sat down at the kitchen table, took off his fedora, and scratched his head as he liked to do. "You stayed at my house?" he asked. "You stayed there?"

"Yes," my grandmother said. "Don't tell me you didn't notice that we ate all your food and slept in your beds."

"I can tell you truthfully," said *Tío* Nano, "that Lina and I didn't notice."

"That's because you must have company all the time," my mother said.

"We never have company," said *Tío* Nano. "Lina is very insecure. You know she's a very private person."

"You mean to tell me," said my grandmother watching *Tío* Nano eat, "that you and Lina didn't notice we had been there?"

"Where?" asked *Tío* Nano.

"Your home," said my mother.

"My home?" asked *Tío* Nano.

"Your home," my mother reminded him. "Your home on Washington."

"On Washington?" *Tío* Nano asked. "Didn't I tell you?"

"No," my mother and grandmother answered, sitting down at the table. "Tell us what?"

Tío Nano eyed the plate of food in front of him. He was only halfway through. He began to eat hurriedly, like a dog. Through mouthfuls, leaning over the plate, he slurred, "We haven't lived in the house on Washington for a year."

"Well, who lives there now? Your son Gil and his wife I hope?" my grandmother asked him.

"I don't know," he replied, giving his plate to my grandmother for some more meat and potatoes. "I just don't know.

A lot of people are moving in and out of Laredo. The economy is very bad." Then he blushed and said, "One more tortilla, please. Just to finish the meat."

In the morning, after a heavy breakfast of *chorizo*, eggs and tortillas, *Tío* Nano gathered his suitcases and left. We were all out on the street and could see him on the road standing between his suitcases, thumbing a ride. My grandmother said, "Next time I'm not coming out of the bathroom. I'm not coming out. It will take horses to drag me out. Does everybody understand? Maybe I should act crazy...like Mercé. Like Pepa. No one bothers them. That's the way to be. Crazy. I've learned my lesson. From now on I'm acting crazy. And I'm getting out of the kitchen. You don't see Mercé and Pepa in the kitchen slaving away, do you?"

"Maybe you can scare him with a knife the next time he comes around," said Cota.

"That won't do it," said my grandmother. "You cannot scare a man away when he's starving. He's like a dog. You can't scare him off. He'll put up with anything just so that he can eat. There is not an insult big enough to run him off. No, the only way to avoid him is to hide."

My mother said, "Well, why do you keep coming out when he shows up? Why can't you stay in hiding?"

"Because," my grandmother replied.

"Because," my mother said, "you're very *metiche*, very nosey."

My grandmother looked at her very sternly and said, "Why don't you mind your own business?"

"Then don't complain," my mother responded, walking away.

Tío Nano was sitting on one of his suitcases. He was cleaning the hat band with his handkerchief. We saw him place his handkerchief up to his mouth to cover a burp. Had we been close we would have smelled the *chorizo*.

"Look at him. He ate so much he's still digesting my breakfast," said my grandmother.

Tío Pacho

Tío Pacho was born Bonifacio Elizondo and lived in Benavides, south of San Diego. He was related to us indirectly. He was my grandfather's uncle, my grandfather's mother's younger brother, and therefore an uncle to everyone of us. He would appear four or five times a year at our doorsteps, a short thin man with his pant legs stuck inside his weathered, lopsided cowboy boots. He had a large head, and on top of it he carried a whirlwind of a crop of hair which he parted down the middle. He had very dark, close-set eyes, like a possum, and glued under his nose was a bushy moustache that looked like a squirrel's tail that kept you from seeing his mouth. To drink his coffee he had to push his moustache up with the index finger of his left hand while he held the cup with his right. Despite this precaution, the tips of the hair under his nose were burnt and stained with coffee and tobacco. Although he had never married, Pacho was always in love.

We were always delighted to see Pacho, for he was not a great eater like *Tío* Nano, although he had the inconsiderate habit of slapping one tortilla at the bottom of his plate before serving himself. That way, when he began eating, he was already on his second tortilla, having squirreled the first under the food. He was a great raconteur and one of the finest liars who ever lived. As soon as we would spy him coming down the street, we would begin talking about him—what magical stories he had for us on this trip, what lies he would tell us that night in the darkness by the old cot that my grandmother would set up for him between the two great salt cedars so that he could sleep out in the open.

"The sounds of the air breezing across the salt cedars," he would sigh, looking to the upper branches of the large trees, "reminds me of the voices of beautiful women. School teachers." For some reason it was always school teachers.

My grandmother would elbow my grandfather in the ribs in the dark, and they would look at each other and then at us, and it was all that we could do to keep from sniggering. Meanwhile *Tío* Pacho, still looking up into the night, would let out another sigh, this time one of nostalgia, that would have been worthy of the greatest of lovers.

And there was always something spectacular, never something ordinary, that had happened to him in his travels.

This time he had arrived with a pair of scissors and a comb in his shirt pocket. Although we had begged him to tell us about the two items, he had refused, ignoring us until my grandfather and my father had come from work and we had all eaten and were properly seated by the cot. He made sure his audience was all there: my grandfather, Gonzalo; my grandmother, María Saenz; my mother, Marillita; my father, Gonzalo, whom *Tío* Pacho called Gonzalito; and then the rest; Cota, Juan, Matías, Maggie, Frances, Richard, Sylvia, and I.

"And the comb and the scissors?" my grandfather led him on.

He looked down thoughtfully and stayed frozen for a few moments, as though the thought of what had happened had overshadowed anything he had ever experienced before. This was a standard beginning for him, and I now feel it was more of a ritual during which he unlocked all the conscious restraints which could interfere with his imagination. Then he began to shake his head slowly as if he could not believe the story himself. He took us all in with the gaze of his little eyes, winking them slowly to moisten them.

"Well," he said, finally, "I come from La Reforma this time, the little ranch where my brother lives. Had been there visiting my brother Manuel for a few days. Helping him out at the grocery store. He was paying me very well. Very well. More than I had a right to expect. Anyway, I was leaning down to pick up a sack of beans when the urge hit me to cut hair. You understand that I had never cut hair before."

Having said that, he quickly realized that he had admitted to something which might make him look bad in our eyes, and like most good liars, he set out to correct his mistake before continuing with the story.

He said, "Well, I take that back. I had cut hair once before when the barber at Benavides became ill from eating

cactus. He blocked his gut. *Empacho.* If you have *empacho*
you'll never grow. This is a dreaded disease for the young."
He eyed all of the children around him. "Don't ever eat cactus," he cautioned. "And if you happen to, well, then drink
mesquite tea. Plenty of it to move your bowels immediately."
We filed that in the back of our minds. Then, comfortable
once more, he continued with the barber from Benavides.

"In those days I was curing people since we had no doctor
to speak of. The people of Benavides brought the barber to
me. I had to prescribe some treatments for him. Enemas.
Drenches of goat milk. That sort of thing."

"What about the tea from the mesquite?" Matías asked.
Hadn't he just prescribed mesquite tea?

Tío Pacho dismissed the question with a wave of his hand
toward Matías. His lying mind was too fast for us. "Too far
gone for mesquite tea," he explained. He stopped and looked
around in the dark to see if we had reacted favorably to the
lie within the lie. He was satisfied that we were properly
impressed.

"Anyway, my brother Manuel says to me that what I need
to cut hair is a chair and a pair of scissors and a comb. No
sooner had he said it, when a pair of scissors and a comb are
found inside the first drawer that I look into. And these were
scissors for cutting hair. Not scissors that the women use for
cutting cloth. The chair was next door in my brother
Manuel's house. A kitchen chair. What do I need a barber's
chair for? So I brought it over and set it on the porch outside
the store. My God, man! In two days I was cutting the hair of
hundreds of men, women and children. My brother Manuel
went to see the priest. Went to see him to see if this was some
form of miracle. The priest came over, and I cut his hair. Just
a few strands, mind you. He was almost bald. Like the priest
in Benavides that has no hair since the incident with the goat
dung."

He readjusted his seat on the cot. "No one," he continued,
"had seen so many people before. And possibly after. Manuel,
my brother, was taking in the money. Bags of money. He was
talking of closing the store and both of us going on the road,
but I cautioned him. 'Easy gains,' I remember telling him,
'are easily lost.' And as God is wont to propose, God is willing
to dispose. By that I mean that the urge to leave struck me in
the middle of a haircut. The mayor. I was cutting the mayor's

hair. His beautiful daughter, a school teacher, sitting right by me watching my every move with the scissors. She admired me greatly and whispered so that the other customers waiting could not hear her. The mayor, her father, frowned at her as though she was lowering herself by talking to me. And I said to the mayor, very sternly, that many a school teacher would give her right arm to be by my side and I could prove it. How many virgin school teachers came to see me the last time I was at La Reforma? When I was playing the harmonica and the guitar at the same time? Well, I tell you the truth. If you want to hear it. That time, my brother Manuel had to keep the virgin school teachers away. Failing at being with me, the virgins proposed to honor me with a banquet. I was telling the mayor all of this, and now the mayor, who had not wanted his daughter to speak to me, was dumbfounded. Did not know what to do. Immediately, I knew what type of person *he* was. A person who thinks he knows it all. Why, had he not been the mayor, I would have fought him right then and there. I would have showed him the pugilistic style of someone like Kid Azteca, my boxer friend from Mexico who I trained at one time, who fought with one hand tied behind his back. Anyway, all this bickering was getting to me. What do I need all this money for when I have all the friends in the world?"

"For nothing," my grandfather replied.

"You don't need the money," my father added.

"Exactly," *Tío* Pacho agreed, leaning over on one buttock to take out his tobacco pouch from his back pocket. In the dark, while we waited, he tapped a small row of tobacco on to a corn shuck. He rolled the shuck and stuck it inside his mouth, completely hidden by the moustache. He pulled the cigarette out slowly, licking it with his tongue. He struck a match and lit the cigarette, causing a flash of light in the darkness as the tip of his moustache caught fire. We laughed silently as he patted the fire out from under his nose. Ignoring his predicament, he took a long drag, used up all the cigarette, and then threw the stub under the cot.

"And then?" my grandmother asked.

"I stopped. Like God Almighty had taken my hand and stopped it, and I could cut hair no more. The mayor gets up and throws the towel at me. I duck like the boxer. He grabs his beautiful daughter by the hand and forces her, almost

throws her, out through the door. The poor girl protested. She
wanted with all her heart to stay near me. That night, before
I departed, my brother Manuel and his friends threw a banquet for me. A meal like you wouldn't believe. They killed
goats and pigs and chickens and calves. All you could hear all
day long were the bleatings of the poor animals protesting
their deaths. I tried to stop them. Feeling sorry for the poor
animals. But what is one man when a mob of friends is set on
something? As a guest of honor, I was seated next to another
school teacher. She sat on my left, an honor for her, I'm sure.
The most beautiful young woman I had ever seen. No,
Gonzalo, the mayor's daughter was ugly in comparison. This
one's hair was like corn silk. Her eyes were jewels. A color
like I had never seen before. Between green and blue. Like
sparkling diamonds. To tell you that her lips were like rubies
would be an injustice. Just seeing her next to me made me
want to faint. She gave me her hand, and I took it and kissed
it. I knew that she wanted to marry me, but how could I, a
poor fellow, encourage someone to ruin their life? Let someone like that marry a rich man. An educated man. A young
man, besides. Not an old fool like me. But she was attracted
to me, she said. Well, I had to tell her a lot of women are
attracted to me. It's in my nature, María. Poor thing. Had I
had a meaner heart, I could have ruined her reputation." He
winked at my grandfather, whose stomach was heaving as he
tried to suppress his laughter.

He gazed at my grandmother, and my grandmother said,
trying to be serious, "Thank God for your honesty, Pacho."

"Pacho, no woman can be safe when you're around," said
my father, egging him on.

"You know the truth, Gonzalito," he said, eyeing my
father seriously, and his small chest seemed to expand with
pride.

"Another man would have taken advantage. I'm sure," my
mother said.

"Sure, he would have," Bonifacio Elizondo reassured us
all. "I know that. And then I left. The following day. My
brother Manuel said for me to take the scissors and the comb.
'You'll be successful again,' he told me. And of that I was
sure. So I began my journey through the ranches. Cutting
hair. Everywhere I went they had a banquet. And at every
banquet there was a school teacher much like the one at La

Reforma. More beautiful than the mayor's daughter at La Reforma, I might add. Word of my travels preceded me. By the time I arrived at a ranch, the crowd would be there. Slowly, I accumulated donations of livestock—horses, mules, cows, chickens, dogs and cats."

Another mistake! He sensed instantly that we were not impressed with dogs and cats. He said, "Well, the dogs and cats I returned. They were of no use to me. Except one. A dog who people claimed could tell the hour of the day. And I saw him do it. Could tell exactly what hour and minute it was, Gonzalo. He would bark out the numbers. But still, I felt compelled to return such a valuable animal. His owner was crying when he offered it to me. By the time I arrived at Benavides, I had accumulated a king's ransom in livestock, having had to ask for donations of wagons and teams of mules to drive them. I was amazed when I looked behind me at the caravan of goods that had been bestowed on me. Everything I touched turned to gold.

"I arrived in Benavides with so much livestock that the neighbors could not believe it. Ultimately I had to give it all away. What else could I do? The people were coming by and admiring everything that I had. I felt unworthy of all the attention. That, coupled with my generosity, was my undoing. So little by little—a chicken here, a calf there, a goat here, a cow there, a horse here, a mule there—I was down to nothing. You know how generous I can be. Ever since I was a child. My mother used to scold me for it. How many marbles did I give away, Gonzalito? Millions! Not to mention spinning tops."

My grandmother was not one to keep quiet. After all, she had fed the man two meals. She said, "And you didn't find it in your heart to save one animal for us, Pacho?"

Tío Pacho caught the nuance. He said, quickly, "You were first in my mind, María. And I saved the best cow for you. She gave so much milk it was hard to keep her udder from bursting. She gave milk on her own. One didn't have to milk her. Just put a pail under her, and in no time it would be full. 'This one is for María and Gonzalo and the children and Marillita and Gonzalito,' I said, thinking about all of you. But as I always say, God proposes and God disposes. The poor cow, just last night, as I was walking her from the pasture, was bitten by a snake as big and long as any I had ever seen.

Tried to swallow the cow after it killed her. But I was able to kill the snake. God forbid it should escape."

"What bad luck," my grandmother said, trying to inject some sadness into her voice. "And here I was thinking that you had given everything to everyone except us."

"Nooooo," *Tío* Pacho said, cocking his little eyes at us and leaning on one buttock as he crossed his leg, "You are foremost on my mind. But luck is luck."

"How unlucky we always are," my mother murmured.

"And where is the money then?" my grandfather wanted to know. "All the money you made cutting hair?"

Not that he was trying to trap the man, he was simply wanting, like the rest of us, to see how *Tío* Pacho would disentangle himself from the story.

Tío Pacho sighed once more, rolled another cigarette and caught his moustache on fire with the large wooden match. After putting out the flames he said, "When one makes money easily, it seems to go out easily. One of the things in life that I have observed. Wine. Women. Song. Parties with school teachers. Gifts. What have you. What do I know? This is why I set myself as an example to other people. My easy gains never enrich me. Let that be a lesson to us all."

"We didn't get to share in any of the money either?" my grandmother cried out to keep from laughing.

"No," *Tío* Pacho said sternly, as though he was answering a child. Then he felt the need to place more woes on his back. "It gets worse." This was really the story my grandfather wanted to hear. He continued, "Then, suddenly, my brother Manuel gets sick. Very sick. He almost died. I don't know if you have heard. He ate a thorn from a mesquite. Playing around. You know how he is. He had this twig in his mouth. Climbing a windmill. He looks down and gets dizzy. You know how he has always suffered from dizziness. Instead of coming down, like an idiot he goes to the top where he gets worse. Finally, when they can get him down, he feels the pain. In his excitement he had swallowed part of the twig and the thorn that went with it. Well, what can I tell you? I had to send him all the rest of my money. What was left. It took that and a banquet to raise money to pay for the doctor. I now have this," he said, leaning over and putting his hand in his pocket. He took out a coin that we could not distinguish in the darkness. He showed it around quickly, before anyone could grab it, and then returned it to his pocket.

In the morning, after my father and grandfather had gone to work, he offered to cut all the children's and the women's hair. The women refused politely, making excuses that matched *Tío* Pacho's imagination. He insisted on cutting the children's hair. He needed to pay for his food and for his keep. My grandmother and mother felt sorry for him and they relented.

He set up a kitchen chair in the middle of the yard and brought out a bowl from the kitchen. He took out his scissors and sniped at the air.

He said, "I can cut a mosquito in half on the fly. But that's another story."

I was listening to him when Juan and Matías picked me up and sat me on the chair. *Tío Pacho* placed the bowl on my head and began to cut my hair, using the bowl for a pattern.

As it was, I was *Tío Pacho's* first and last victim. When the others saw what a job he was doing on me, they took off for the cave at the creek. Only when they were sure the coast was clear of *Tío Pacho* did they come out for air again.

Mercé

Tío Mercé lived with us, setting him apart from the large
group of uncles who would come by to get a handout meal or
a cup of coffee—*tío*s like Adolfo, Nano, Juanito Everett,
Gumercindo, Manuel Saenz, and Pacho. He would be the last
to eat, my grandmother saving little bits and pieces from
everyone's plate to complete a meal for him while he waited
patiently outside, sitting by the kitchen door. He slept at his
mother's old abandoned house on the corner, an old unpaint-
ed house whose wood had turned gray and had grown a vel-
vet-like covering as soft as a peach. He had one kerosene lantern to light his way around the house, but we never saw him
use it. He must have realized that it was dangerous for him
to light a fire. So Mercé slept in complete and shadowless
darkness. When we went looking for him at night, we had to
feel our way against the wall until we found, on the right, the
closed door to his room. We could smell his presence in the
darkness when we opened the door, the smell of Bugler, of
Bull Durham, the cheap tobacco which he burned in cigarettes rolled in corn husks, of the stale yeast of beer he drank
which permeated his body

After a week or so of being close to him, my grandmother
would ask him to take a bath. She would take out some clean
clothes for him, and he would bathe in the shed behind the
house where we had a shower that drained under the floor
and into the back yard.

My grandmother, who in her innocence believed everything that happened had a cause or a cure, had an explanation for Mercé's affliction. She believed Mercé had drank a
potion meant for someone else in a beer. Some scorned
woman had meant to chemically castrate her man by lacing

his beer, and Mercé, as a result, had lost his manhood. His naturalness, she called it, had never descended, whatever that meant. "You know what I mean, don't you?" she would ask, and we would all nod our little heads, wondering what she was talking about, no one wanting to ask and be the fool. Cota was the most astute of the bunch and even she could not explain to the rest of us what "undescended naturalness" meant. "It probably has something to do with his *huevos*," she would say and then dismiss the conversation and talk about something else. Juan and Matías would laugh, and then my brother and sister and I would go along with them to the creek to play and smoke, not thinking at all of the disease which afflicted Mercé. To us he was normal, except for those times, and we could forget them very easily.

"His naturalness is still in his head," my grandmother would explain, and we would go along with the theory. "If a man's naturalness does not descend, it stays in his head and he goes crazy."

"How do you know?" asked Matías.

"I just do," she would say, and that was the end of that.

So only María Saenz knew what she was talking about, and I'm sure it pleased her knowing no one would question her theory.

The truth was, undescended naturalness or not, Mercé was insane. He could be sitting down at the table or sitting outside whittling or rolling a cigarette and he would start to mumble. And then the mumbling would get worse, louder. He would shoot up, stare into space and begin to curse, softly at first, gathering momentum in time until he could be heard from blocks away. He would grab the lobes of his ears and yank them violently, as though some demon were inside his brain. He would do this over and over until it seemed he would never stop, until blood would come out of his ears, until we were afraid he would tear them off. If this happened in the small kitchen while we were all eating, there would be a small commotion with us trying to get out of his way as best we could and my grandmother shouting at him, trying to make him behave. Of course, she couldn't. Invariably, he would run into the streets, sometimes in the direction of the rectory and the convent where the priest and the nuns had been watching him from the window. The Mother Superior would hurry through the convent, closing the shutters to protect the sensitive ears of the younger nuns. Father Zavala, jaded from having to carry the burden of the sins from so many confessions, would merely walk away to the far side of the house so that he would not appear to have noticed. If we were around, my grandmother would yell at us to go catch him, try to turn him around toward the house, and bring him back. If we weren't there, he would travel as far as the seizure would take him, sometimes clear to the other end of town, and he would take several hours to return.

My sister Sylvia hated to bring her friends from school to the house because of Mercé. She lived in fear of embarrassment that he would go into a fit around one of her friends who did not know him. All the rest of us—Cota, Maggie, Frances, Juan, Matías, Richard and myself—didn't care. We liked to be around him. There was never a dull moment.

One day the inevitable happened. Two of Sylvia's classmates came by uninvited to see her after school. We were all showing off, behaving ourselves for once, sitting at the porch at my grandmother's house drinking tea when Mercé, freshly showered, his hair wet and plastered down, came out of the shed at a full trot, yanking at his ears and shouting obscenities. He ran past us without as much as giving us a look, took off into the street, and this time headed straight for the Luby house, a three-story mansion which belonged to the cattle and land baron, Jason Luby. Mercé ran into the fence and kept pushing against it, shouting obscenities at old Mrs. Luby. Mrs. Luby was peeking out through a window, watching a deranged man crashing against her fence and shouting things about her which surely weren't true. She never seemed to mind, however. She was used to seeing Mercé having insane fits, cursing her and other people in town. She died at a good age, but no telling how much longer she would have lasted without the barrage of insults.

Unfortunately, my sister Sylvia's friends had never seen Mercé have a fit, and when he passed by them at a trot, yelling his obscenities, they screamed and hid under the old wicker sofa my grandmother had moved from the living room to the porch and where she sat at night rubbing camphorated alcohol on her arms and neck. My sister Sylvia tried to calm her friends, but to no avail. The two girls crawled around under the sofa until they got stuck and we had to lift it to free them. They jumped up, dusted themselves, still screaming in horror at what they had just seen and heard, and ran off as fast as Mercé had done, but in the opposite direction, toward the convent and the protection of the nuns. Shortly afterwards, my sister Sylvia told my brother Richard and me that she could never get married as long as Mercé was alive. She was seven at the time and thinking ahead.

All of San Diego knew Mercé and knew of his affliction. He was accepted as part of the local cast of characters. Many times, Mercé would have a fit in the middle of town and run down the little main street, in and out of the C.O.D. Bar, through the pool hall and back out into the street, and no one even bothered to look at him. Most of the men were more interested in what *Tío* Amando had to say as he held court in front of the butcher shop.

When he was a young man, Mercé had worked as a wrangler for the Lubys. He would come by for me on his horse, place me in front of the saddle, and together we would ride into town. When he had a fit, the horse, used to it by then, would duck his head and move his ears around quickly like antennas, trying to find a position that would keep him from the full blast of Mercé's obscenities. The Lubys let him go. He was cursing the grand old lady too much.

Dr. Dunlap got us an appointment and we took him one Friday to the insane asylum in San Antonio to see what could be done for him. He had two fits in the car, brought on, I suppose, by the thought of being separated from us. My grandmother, riding up front with my mother and father, begged us to control him, but we couldn't. He kicked and scratched to try to get to his ears until the fits ended. The doctors insisted on keeping him, wanting to study his insanity. We were very depressed on the way back, hardly talking to each other. My grandmother was crying, saying she would have never brought him if she had known they were going to keep him.

After one month we missed him so much that we returned to the asylum to try to get him back.

When we drove in through the gate, we saw Mercé sitting on a bench rolling a cigarette. We yelled when we saw him. My father began to honk the horn. Mercé recognized us and came running. He jumped in the car and wouldn't get out. So my father drove around the circular drive and came back out on the street and we never looked back. We didn't talk to the doctors. It turned out to be the right decision. According to

Mercé, the doctor's were not doing anything for him except watching him run around the grounds having fits. He came back fatter, but soon lost his weight running around town cursing everyone with seemingly renewed vigor.

In his older years he would sit around the yard whittling, talking to himself and smoking. When he got tired of that, he would take off for the taverns.

My father bought him a cow to take care of, to give him some responsibilities. Mercé enjoyed the cow. He would milk her in the mornings and then take her out through town looking for an empty lot with grass where he could put her out to pasture. Then he would go to the tavern where he would spend the day drinking what was offered to him. In the meantime, he would have a fit or two. Later, he would pick up the cow on his way home, staggering down the road, the animal anxiously leading him, her udder bursting with milk. We would then give him a hand with the milking, holding the lantern by the pail so that he could see better in his drunken state.

Some nights Mercé would return without the cow, having either forgotten about her or not remembering where he had left her. We would all go with my father and him to look for her, happy that we had something exciting to do at night and listening to the overlapping of the night sounds—the piercing wails of the dying locusts, the cowbell ringing in the hollowness of the dark, a solitary dog barking at a shadow somewhere. Then we would take up a favorite game, the counting of a hundred fireflies, while we sifted the still warm sand between our toes as we walked.

After the Lubys took the horse away from Mercé, he enjoyed taking me out for walks to town, holding my hand and, when he sensed me tiring, carrying me in his arms. When his fits got so bad that he could not keep control of me, my mother told him he could not take me any more. My mother was afraid he was going to drop me on my head during one of his fits and hurt me. And besides, I was hearing too many obscenities at too young an age.

When I got older, my father would lend us his old single shot .22 and we would go hunting together. We never killed anything. During his fits he would scare off all the animals around for miles and besides, it was not in his nature to kill. When we saw a rabbit, I would point it out to him. He would keep on walking and say, "We'll kill him on the way back." We would walk for as long as he felt I should go and not be tired.

"See, Mercé," I would say. "We never kill anything if we wait until we come back."

"We'll kill him tomorrow," he would say. Then when we returned, the rabbit was never there.

When I would come home late at night on college vacations, Mercé would be waiting for me early the next morning. I would go out and sit with him and we would talk about little things. When I asked him how he felt, how he was doing, he always answered "*bien,*" that he was doing well. He never complained about the life he had brought him—his insanity. Acceptance ruled his life. His sane moments were so serene and calm that a stranger would have easily picked him out as the only sane person among a sea of relatives always in turmoil.

The cow had died by then and he had been left with no responsibilities. He was drinking more than ever. The last morning I spent with him, he got up as we spoke, started his fit, and ran away. Feeling it would be insulting to him for me to try to stop him, I let him go.

Inside my grandmother's house I saw the cot where he slept—she had moved him over to her house to keep a closer watch on him, to make sure he didn't die alone after he had discarded Dr. Dunlap's advice about not drinking. That was at Christmas, a sad time for all of us. But, I had thought then, what does a person like Mercé, the disfranchised among us, care about Christmas?

Shortly after I returned to school, my mother called to tell me Mercé had died. She did not want me taking time off from my studies to come to the funeral.

"He would have understood," she said. "It's too far to come and too much trouble."

This time Dr. Dunlap had insisted that he have no liquor. He was not allowed outside the house. In a few days he was dead. As courageous as he was, he could not stand to live a sober life.

Of Sows and Hemorrhoids

My grandfather had farmed in the north part of the county and even farther to the west, toward Freer, almost to the ranch called *Siete Hermanas*. He farmed mostly grain sorghum—Hygeia we called it then, not realizing that was the name of the company which produced the seed. He farmed a few acres of watermelons. We would eat watermelons at night, still hot from the day-long sun, ripping the heart of the fruit out with our bare hands. He raised peanuts one year, and since we had never before seen peanuts grow, he took us to the field one day and told us to pick all the peanuts we could find, gather them, and bring them in to check our crop. We never found any, not knowing they grew underground, and he laughed so much at us and told the story on us afterwards for many years until he died of a heart attack at the meat market.

In spite of my grandmother's worrying about him, he agreed with farming—share-cropping like he always did—with Mr. Gallagher, an old man from Alice who had a few acres to the south of San Diego. Mr. Gallagher, as he insisted that we call him, didn't farm. He enjoyed raising the big fat hogs that were so popular in those days, hogs so big it took three men with rifles to kill one—one each to shoot at the side of the skull and one to shoot at the forehead at the point in the cross where the two lines from the eye to the opposite ear bisect; hogs that must have weighed seven hundred pounds; that were bigger than four men; that lay about in the mud eating left over trash Mr. Gallagher fed them. Of all his pigs, Mr. Gallagher loved his sows most. He loved them more than his family.

One time he tried to kill a boar by himself when we weren't around so he wouldn't have to share, and instead of killing the hog, he almost killed himself. He took out his twenty-two rifle and tried to shoot the animal, and the boar went crazy, angry at someone who would be pestering him with little bits of pain. It attacked Mr. Gallagher, pinned him face down in the mud, and then sat on him. If we hadn't come by when we heard the squeals of disgust from the hog, Mr. Gallagher would have died in the pig pen. So he learned his lesson, and he would ask us to help him—something we didn't like doing since we were sharecropping. And we knew Mr. Gallagher was going to bring his son Hebert with him from Alice and that we were only going to get a few pounds of pork skin.

"You Mexicans don't like meat anyway," he would say.

"You'd be surprised," my grandfather would answer.

Mr. Gallagher liked to speak Spanish to us although we all understood English, especially my grandfather, who had a good vocabulary. But Mr. Gallagher enjoyed speaking in Spanish, remembering, I'm sure, the old days when, as he liked to brag, he had ten Mexicans working for him on a ranch in Beeville. His problem was that, because Spanish is a language which depends so much on gender, when someone who only has a casual knowledge of the language speaks it and confuses the gender, it not only irritates the ear, but it also offends the soul. And not wanting to correct the old man constantly, we would just walk away from him and nod our heads. We would leave him standing there wondering if we had understood or not. "¿Comprenda?" he would ask, using the wrong word ending again as we walked away. He never realized that it was easier for us to communicate in English than it was for him to speak Spanish. But I suppose he felt superior to us using Spanish. That would make him completely bilingual, smarter. We were not supposed to know English.

Mr. Gallagher came over one day when we were out in the field, and he stopped my grandfather in his tractor and informed us he had just sold the old boar, the one that had almost killed him. We looked over to the pig pen in the distance and saw the men running out in the field, chasing the old boar, trying to catch him and load him. By the time we left for home, when we went by the pig pen, all we saw were the sows and the damage the boar had done to the pig pen. We could see where the big hog had ripped off boards and had escaped. There were tire marks on the ground where the driver had spun his wheels, dragging the boar across the yard from the little house by the fence. They were forced to load up the boar in the open field. We could see where the loading door from the trailer had dragged across several rows.

Mr. Gallagher didn't show up the morning of the next day, and my grandfather worried about him. We were sitting under a mesquite, eating our lunch when we saw the dust from the old pick-up coming up the road. "There he is," my grandfather said. "I wonder why he's so late?"

We waited in the shade as Mr. Gallagher drove over to where we hid from the noon-day sun. He drove under the shade, got off, and greeted us all.

"What happened to you?" my grandfather asked him.

Mr. Gallagher looked down, spat, and said, "It's my brother'n San Antonio. He's had a heart aaattack. I gotta go see 'im. *Muy mala.*"

"*Malo,*" Juan corrected him.

"Is he dying?" my grandfather asked, ignoring Juan.

"No," Mr. Gallagher replied, "he's doint fine, but I has to go see 'im. You know how it is wis' brothers. "

"And you want us to take care of the pigs," Matías said.

"Well, yes," Mr. Gallagher answered. "It weren't be too much trouble. Just get some slop and throw it at 'em. I'll be back in two days. "

And with that he touched the brim of his hat and said, "*Adios, amigas.* "

"*Amigas* is for the girls," said Cota.

"What about us?" asked Matías.

"*Amigos, amigas,* whatever," Mr. Gallagher replied, and got into the truck and took off.

My grandfather had been riding the tractor every day for a week without rest, trying to plant his watermelons, riding in the hard iron seat, eight, ten, twelve hours a day. He felt the twinge at first, and then the pain hit him. He stopped the tractor in the middle of the row and cried out for us to go help him off. We carried him to the old Dodge truck, the one without doors, and took him home where he soaked his rear end in cool water. He came out of the bathroom, a towel wrapped around his waist, stooped, barely able to walk, and he looked at my grandmother and said, disgusted, as he climbed into the bed, "It's the hemorrhoids. This time it's bad. "

He spent the next day in bed, watching us through the window screen as we played outside his room. During the night he tossed in pain and was not able to sleep. He got up at three in the morning, ran some water in the tub, and sat in it until daybreak. By then he was so exhausted, he was able to come to the bed and fall asleep.

That night I slept with my grandfather. He was resting more comfortably, but still in quite a lot of pain, when we were awakened by the scratching on the window screen.

"Gonzalo?" I could hear the voice whisper.

"What is it?" my grandfather asked.

"It's me," I heard the voice say.

It was Mr. Gallagher on the way home from San Antonio. My grandfather was awake now and asked who it was.

"Mr. Gallagher," came the reply from the dark.

"What do you want?" my grandfather inquired.

"*Las almorranas ... ¿cómo están?*" he asked my grandfather. "The hemorrhoids...how are they?"

The problem is communicating in two languages. It just so happens that the word in Spanish for hemorrhoids is *almorranas*. The word for sows is *marranas*. Two fairly close words. Mr. Gallagher thought he was asking about his sows when he was asking about hemorrhoids.

"Horrible," my grandfather replied in Spanish, fresh in the thought of his affliction. "In lots of pain...lots of pain. More pain than I've ever seen in my life. "

"*¿Qué pasa?*" the surprised Mr. Gallagher asked in a panic, wondering what had happened to his sows.

"I don't know," my grandfather continued his tale of woe and pain. "It just happened. Lots of blood...pain...not able to walk...eat. Horrible...Wish that death would come. "

My grandfather could not see past the window screen, but Mr. Gallagher was holding on to the window sill, trying not to collapse from the news. All his dearest sows were sick, in pain, bleeding, not eating, waiting for death. He was holding his head down, sobbing gently so that my grandfather could not hear a grown man cry.

"*Vida muy duro,*" we heard Mr. Gallagher proclaim.

"*Dura,*" my grandfather corrected him immediately.

"*Dura...duro*, whatever," Mr. Gallagher answered through the stream of tears.

And my grandfather, not to be outdone in the field of complaint, said in Spanish, "You never know what life brings. But there is no calamity which doesn't bring some good with it. "

"What are we to do?" Mr. Gallagher cried out.

"Wait," my grandfather replied, "Wait and see if time will heal. What else can one do when God sends an affliction?"

Later, we blamed my grandfather also. He should have known Mr. Gallagher was asking about his sows and not about my grandfather's hemorrhoids. It only stands to reason. How could Mr. Gallagher have known about the hemorrhoids? He had just driven into town. But then we had to consider, in my grandfather's defense, that a severe attack of hemorrhoids doesn't allow for much critical thinking.

Mr. Gallagher gathered himself and said, "¡*No más*! Don't say no more. I'm ruint," leaving us in a state of confusion, walking away crying.

"And he left crying," my astounded grandfather told my grandmother in the morning.

"Crying?" my grandmother asked. "Over your hemorrhoids?"

My grandfather got up and felt much better, but not before thinking of Mr. Gallagher and saying to my grandmother, "He must like us after all. "

We were eating breakfast outside in the yard between the two houses early in the morning. Juan and Matías were sitting at one side of the table. Across from them were Cota, Maggie, and Frances. My brother and sister and I were across from our grandfather, who sat alone.

"You see, children," he said. "One must not judge a man by what he appears to be. Wait until you are ill, and then see who your friends are. Surely Mr. Gallagher has proved to be a friend. Who would have thought?"

We were agreeing with him when we heard someone driving a truck at a great rate of speed, crashing gears, spinning its wheels. We looked toward the street and saw Mr. Gallagher's truck. It was him traveling as fast as the old truck would go. He came closer and closer until we felt he might not stop, might want to run over all of us. In a desperate act, we ran to hide behind the salt cedars in the yard, looking for protection from a man gone mad. Finally, when we were sure he was going to run into the table out in the yard, he slammed on the brakes at the driveway and slid cross-wise toward us, leaning the truck on its side before coming to a stop. Mr. Gallagher got off, and pointing a finger at my grandfather, began to say something. But in his anger, the only sounds we could hear were squeaks and grunts and moans. He tried several times, but he could not speak. We later knew he had come from visiting his sows. He calmed down a bit, and when he could open his mouth he said, "Everyone off'n my land. I don't want to see none of you on my land...ever again." He ran to the truck, got in, and took off in as big a hurry as he had arrived.

We looked at each other and wondered what had gotten into the old man. My grandfather gathered us all and we drove in the old Dodge truck without the doors to Alice to inform Mr. Gallagher's wife that the old man had lost his senses.

We found Mrs. Gallagher in the shade of a hackberry in the back yard shelling peas for dinner, a little black and white dog at her feet waiting for a stray pea to fall its way. She took the news calmly. We didn't know at the time that she was a hypochondriac when it came to Mr. Gallagher's health. She put down her bowl of peas and got up and walked slowly to the house. Looking back at us she said, "I told 'im he'd either have a heart aaattack one of these days like his brother done done or go crazy some day...him and 'is hogs. You cain't love a hog more'n your wife and not go crazy. "

"Where are you going?" my grandfather asked her.

"To telephlome his son Hebert," she replied. "We'll go fetch him. He needs to be brung home and placed in a hospital like I always prae..dicted. "

When we all got back to San Diego, we found Mr. Gallagher in the pig pen on his knees hugging his sows. His son Hebert got to him first, and being a big man, he picked up the confused and startled Mr. Gallagher like one would pick up a scarecrow and forcibly threw him over the pen where his wife was waiting for him. She jumped on him, and between the two of them and us helping, ignoring his cries, we were able to tie him up and get him into the back seat of the car, and his wife and son drove off with him to take him to the hospital in Corpus Christi.

This tragedy really put a burden on us. Now we had the sows to feed and take care of besides finishing planting our watermelons. But our grandfather said that we should count our blessings. How would we like to be insane like Mr. Gallagher? Well, we had seen what an insane man acts like, and we knew it wouldn't be any fun. He had been worse than Mercé. We'd rather plant watermelons.

A day later we see the dust from Mr. Gallagher's truck coming up the road. My grandfather told us not to talk to him, that he might be dangerous. We didn't have to say anything because Mr. Gallagher didn't say a word to us. He kept to himself. Whenever we'd go by in the old Dodge truck without the doors, we'd greet him, but he would look the other way, a scowl implanted permanently on his face.

One night I woke up with the bed shaking. I called to my grandfather, but he didn't answer. I turned on the light and saw him turning blue, his whole body trembling. I was in a panic. I ran to go get my grandmother and woke her up. Cota, Maggie, Frances, and Sylvia were sleeping with her. In the next room, Matías and Juan heard the noise and got up. We all ran back into his bedroom. My grandfather was sitting up, shaking, not able to breathe, having a laughing fit. In a state of lucidness, in between dreams, he had finally figured out what Mr. Gallagher was asking about that night and he could not control himself.

"Mr. Gallagher doesn't know the difference between hemorrhoids and sows," he was barely able to say between the laughter.

"At three o'clock in the morning you figure it out?" my grandmother complained.

The next day my grandfather approached Mr. Gallagher cautiously, and from a safe distance spoke to him and told him the difference.

Mr. Gallagher thought a few moments as he continued to rub his favorite sow between the eyes, and said, "Spanish is the hardest language there is to learnt. "

The next year, still hurt from the incident, he let my grandfather have less acreage so that we couldn't plant watermelons. My grandfather, just to get even, planted gourds and when Mr. Gallagher asked him what we were doing, my grandfather took a dried gourd we were using for seed and shook it at him. We started dancing to the rhythm of the gourd. My grandfather said, dancing, "We are going to get rich selling *maracas* for dancing. And don't confuse them with *marranas*.

"I'll never understand Mexican talking," Mr. Gallagher said, walking away.

The Cushions

We lost track of my grandfather for a while after he went to San Antonio to find a job. Then one day when we went to the post office, we found a letter. Cota turned the knob on the box to the three numbers in our combination and flipped the handle. She reached inside as all of us waited to see who it was from. Cota read the return address out loud, and it was him. We ran home, Cota waving the letter as she ran up front.

When we arrived, my grandmother was rinsing beans, standing at the sink, looking at us through the open kitchen window. She had watched us running down the street, wondering what we were shouting about. "What is it?" she laughed when we crossed the street and ran into the yard. "You children act like you've found a treasure."

Cota waved the letter at her. "It's father," she cried out.

The letter was short. My grandfather had found a job in San Antonio working at a liquor store on the east side on Commerce Street.

"My God," my grandmother worried out loud, covering her mouth with her fingers, "that's the bad part of town...and he's getting old."

"He says that he has to work until ten and gets up at five in the morning," Matías read over Cota's shoulder.

"Heaven forbid," my grandmother objected, "the poor man doesn't get to sleep...But," she reasoned after a short pause, "he has always been an early riser. Never liked to stay in bed."

"He's staying with Suzy," Maggie read out loud.

"At least that's good," my grandmother replied.

"And," Cota kept on, studying the letter, "he's sending us something that he bought for the house."

One week later when we went on our daily post-office run, we saw the little slip of paper that Mr. Amaya had placed in our box. We fought to get to it, until Juan stopped the struggle and shoved everyone out of the way, including Matías. Very slowly and deliberately, he turned the knob and then opened the little door to the box. "See," he said, "see how easy it is when we don't fight." He waved the slip of paper over his head, and Cota jumped up and grabbed it from him. She read it. Mr. Amaya had scribbled on it. We had a package from San Antonio. We ran with the slip to the window and Mr. Amaya took it from us and disappeared while we waited. Mr. Amaya then showed up with a large package, not heavy, but large. As usual, we ran home with it. By the time we arrived home, my grandmother, who had seen us running with the package, was outside, eagerly waiting for us. "A package!" she cried out when we arrived. "How beautiful. I love to open packages...God knows I don't get to do it very often. But if you notice, God doesn't give us what we love. Very contrary...that's Him."

My grandfather had sent two silk cushions which, according to Juan, were from a pawn shop. They were slightly used and oily, made in Japan, each with a scene from an oriental forest, with an arching bridge crossing over running water, a large tree with branches overhanging the water, rocks on the shore, and a pagoda in the background. One had a Japanese couple, walking away from us into the cushion, embracing, the lady carrying an umbrella at her side, the man wearing a dress like the woman and wooden shoes. We found the whole scene hilarious.

"What's gotten into your father?" my grandmother wondered as she flipped the cushions, studying them from different angles. "These have been used," she decided after careful inspection, not having wanted to offend my grandfather's taste without being certain.

Not only didn't my grandmother like the cushions, they didn't fit anywhere. If one sat down with them to support the back, they were too thick. And after awhile, whoever was sitting with them would reach back in desperation, take the cushion and fling it across the sofa to the other side where it would roll into the other cushion. Then, like normal children, whoever was sitting on the opposite end of the sofa would throw the cushion back, and this would keep on and on until my grandmother kicked us out of the house.

So Cota, who was our spiritual leader, decided that we ought to raffle the cushions. She thought that the cushions would be a curiosity in San Diego, that we would have no problem selling raffle chances, and we could get money and get rid of the cushions at the same time.

The harder we tried to sell chances on the cushions, the more we realized that a lot of people already owned a set of them. They were being sent home by servicemen stationed in Hawaii before the war.

So one morning, bright and early, Cota tells us that she's decided people who had money were at the courthouse, where George Parr and his cronies hung around, and that that's where we ought to be selling chances on the raffle.

"You want to make money?" she asked us. Of course we did. So off to the courthouse we ran, carrying our cushions with us. But halfway there Matías complained that we couldn't sell anything if we showed people the cushions. So back we went with the cushions, explaining to my grandmother why we weren't going to take them.

"That's smart," she agreed. "I just don't know what got into your father. He's always been the most sensible one in the family." She shook her head and said, "Being away from home, probably."

At the courthouse, we greeted the jailer then separated, Cota sending us in different directions, so that by noon-time when the siren at the fire-station sounded, its wail announcing to the town that it was time to eat, we had gathered outside and had sold two dollars worth of tickets. Cota took the names and the money from us and put the little slips of paper and the coins in her pocket. "This is fun," Frances said, watching Cota put the slips and the money away.

"There's more money in the courthouse than we can count," Cota reminded us.

On the way back, Matías said he was thirsty and he hadn't had a red soda in years. Juan said he wanted one and before we knew it we had changed directions, from going home to going toward town. At *Tacho's*, the drug store, we each got a red soda and sat at the back steps and drank it,

watching the drunks go into the C.O.D. Bar through the back
door so the townspeople wouldn't see them.

We enjoyed ourselves so much that every day we would
go to the courthouse, come back by way of *Tacho's,* and sit at
the back and drink our red sodas.

By Thursday we had run out of money.

When my grandmother asked us where all this money we
bragged about was, Cota told her she had it, was keeping it
herself so we would learn the responsibility of handling
money, to which my grandmother said, "That's very good. I
want all of you to learn to keep your money. God never gives
one enough."

At that instant, my sister and my brother and I thanked
God our mother had called us for supper from across the
yard. Rather than be accomplices to the lie, we ran immediately to our house next door, surprising our mother.

On Friday we went back to the courthouse and tried to
sell more chances for the raffle, but the courthouse cronies
had gotten impatient. They wanted to know when the raffle
was going to take place. "Tomorrow," Cota informed everyone. "Saturday. Tomorrow is the raffle." And when the people
asked us how they would know who won, Cota and Juan and
Matías informed them that we would be by on Monday with
the winner and the cushions.

Monday morning, early, when my sister and my brother
and I got to my grandmother's house, we found Cota, Juan,
Matías, Maggie, and Frances huddled at the rear of the
house, discussing something. When we approached them,
they greeted us and we took off for the courthouse, without
the cushions.

"The cushions?" my sister Sylvia asked, thinking she had
remembered something everyone else forgot.

"Be quiet," Cota replied as she walked up front.

Just outside of the courthouse we stopped and Cota gath-
ered us together in a circle. "This is what we say," she said.
"Everyone listen. Repeat after me...The winner was Mrs.
Garza from Laredo. Say it."

We all repeated the information. The winner was Mrs.
Garza from Laredo.

"That's all there is to it," Cota said. "It's very easy. The
winner was Mrs. Garza from Laredo. That's all you have to

say. If anyone asks anything else, just tell them you don't know."

"But..." my brother started to say.

"No buts," Cota replied. "The winner was Mrs. Garza from Laredo. That's all you say."

We went through the heavy wooden courthouse doors and inside, in the hallway, was George B. Parr, the political king of Texas, talking to his friends. He turned around when he saw us come in and greeted us. "How's the raffle going?" he wanted to know.

Cota walked up to him like she owned the courthouse and replied, "The winner was Mrs. Garza from Laredo."

"Good for her," George B. Parr replied and kept on talking to the men in the group. Then he thought about something and turned around and asked, "What was she doing in San Diego?"

"She was here," Cota said, without missing a beat, "to visit her cousin."

"What family does she belong to?" He was curious to know.

"The Garza's that live by the creek," Cota replied, knowing that the people by the creek were not well known in town.

"Oh," he replied and kept on talking to his friends.

If we could convince him, we figured, we could convince anyone. So buoyed by the confidence that that encounter gave us, we went through the courthouse like a pack of rats shouting the good news that a certain Mrs. Garza from Laredo had won the cushions.

We raffled the cushions several more times, each time having a different winner from out of town and making less and less money. Finally, we had to give up the scheme when we had no more takers. We were stuck with the cushions, and my grandmother, not knowing what we had done, had to take them out to the little shed in the backyard and store them in a box just in case my grandfather should show up unexpectedly.

"I can't believe," she said, trying to figure out where to put the box with the cushions, "that you children could not raffle the cushions. That was the longest raffle I have ever seen. God must not have wanted it." Then she said, scratching her head, "What happened to the money you said you had?"

Cota looked at us and said, "We gave it back."

"At least you did something right," my grandmother grunted from inside the shed as she moved her junk around to make room for the cushions.

"We can always raffle them again next year," Juan reminded her.

"God would kill us all," my grandmother replied, coming out of the shed and looking up to the heavens. "You know how He is."

Six months later my grandfather arrived in an old Dodge truck without doors. In the truck bed he had two goats he had bought at the goat auction in San Antonio. My grandmother, shelling beans, had not recognized him in the truck, and, finally, when she did, when my grandfather stopped in front of the house, she remembered the cushions and ran out to the shed while my grandfather untied the goats. We saw her running back inside the house, hiding the cushions tight against her body.

He had come home to stay. The first thing he asked for when he stepped into the house was the cushions, and my grandmother showed them to him, resting at each end of the sofa. "That's the only thing I could afford at the time," he said. "I'm glad all of you liked them so much." And we were quiet as he thought about something for while, and what he remembered made him take out his handkerchief and wipe a tear from his eye.

He had lost his job. Shortly afterwards he disappeared again.

We Look for My Grandfather

It was my grandmother's brother, *Tío* Gumecindo, who came to talk to her about my grandfather. She had seen the tall and lanky Gumecindo through the kitchen window, the same spot where she had worn out the linoleum looking out for us. She had known *Tío* Gumecindo had news from the way he walked—fast and determined, taking great strides, his hat bouncing with every heavy step he took. She instinctively turned around and faced us as we sat at the kitchen table eating our noon meal. She walked over to the table, wiping her hands on her apron. She said, "It's Gumecindo...he's got something on his mind."

"About father," Cota said, placing a piece of tortilla in her mouth.

"Yes," my grandmother said so heavily that we thought she would have to sit. She grabbed the back of the chair where Juan was sitting. She repeated, "About your father."

Gumecindo struggled with the stuck kitchen screen door, and when he finally was able to force it open, he came right in without knocking. He left the kitchen door open and sat down. Without saying a word, my grandmother reached into the cupboard and brought out a cup and saucer and served him coffee. He took off his hat, crossed his leg and hung the hat on his knee. He pushed his hair back with his fingers and smiled at all of us. "Well, sister," he began as he brought the cup to his mouth, "he's at the *Rancho Grande*."

"I knew it," my grandmother replied. Gumecindo saying it confirmed what she had thought all along. She knew it was my grandfather's favorite place when he had troubles on his mind.

Gumecindo couldn't cool down the coffee. He poured it onto the saucer, blew on it, and began to slurp. "He's doing fine," he continued, eyeing the food.

"Are you hungry?" my grandmother asked *Tío* Gumercindo when she took notice of him.

Gumecindo looked at the food on the table, and no sooner had begun to say that the town siren had no sounded noon yet, when the lone fireman at the station turned the crank on the siren, setting off its wailing noise. Next came Father Zavala's contribution to the noise—the noon bell. *Tío* Gumecindo took out his watch, looked at it at arm's length, and then returned it to his pocket. He got closer to the table, put his hat under the chair, and said, "Now I can eat."

That evening when my father drove in from work, my grandmother called him over. She had been sitting on the porch on the wicker sofa, rubbing her arms and the back of her neck with camphorated alcohol. We were sitting on the porch, enjoying the coolness of the concrete floor. My mother looked out from next door through the kitchen window and came out when she saw my father walking over to my grandmother. She walked over to the porch and got there just as the conversation was beginning.

"Have you found him?" my mother asked as she approached.

"Yes," my grandmother replied. "Gumecindo came today to tell me he's at the *Rancho Grande*."

"How awful," my mother said.

"Well," my grandmother answered, "what can one do? Poor man has lost his job. He can't farm anymore. I know how horrible he must feel."

My father said, "I can go get him."

And my grandmother stopped to think about it for a while as we studied her, waiting for her reply. She pursed her lips in thought and then said, "I don't know. I don't want to hurt him."

Several days later, when my grandfather had not returned, not only did my grandmother want to go get him, she insisted that all of us go with her. So when my father arrived from work, we were all ready to go. We squeezed into the car and drove to the *Rancho Grande,* going north across the bridge on the Benavides highway.

Right after the bridge, my father turned the car to the right into the *caliche* driveway and my grandmother said, "There's the truck." She had been the first to see my grandfather's old truck without doors parked off by itself. Then she said to my father, "Drive around slowly. I don't want him to see us."

My father drove in first gear, the car making a groaning sound, jolting us around inside. He drove to the side of the building next to the parked cars and we could see the men inside through the windows, talking and drinking beer. The car went around to the back, and there we saw a drunk man and a woman arguing. My mother could not stand it. She wanted to go home, but my father kept driving around the building to the other side. Here there were no cars parked and we could pull close to the building. We drove slowly peering inside through the windows at the men and women sitting around having a good time. At the front of the building my father stopped the car, and we could look through the double doors. There in the middle of the dance floor was my grandfather, dancing with a woman, a stranger, dressed in gaudy clothes and wearing lots of make-up. We looked at my grandmother to see what reaction she would have. At first she put her hand up to her mouth as though stifling a sound, but then she regained her composure and looked about, showing some interest.

"Do they charge for men to come to places like this?" she asked innocently.

We hated to find her in a degrading situation such as this. We were used to seeing her always completely in command.

"No," my father replied.

"They ought to," my grandmother replied when she heard my father's answer. "As many people who like to come here."

We could see my grandfather dancing a waltz with the woman, laughing away his cares from having lost his job at the Travelers Hotel in Alice. That had been the last straw.

"He needs a shave," my grandmother said, and we almost laughed.

"Do you want me to go get him?" my father asked my grandmother.

"You should go," my mother said. "He's making a fool of himself and the family."

My grandmother thought for a long time, and when my father grasped the door handle and turned it she reached over and stopped him, saying, "Leave him alone. It would embarrass him to have you go and take him out. He's been embarrassed enough...losing his job. Let him have his fun. Soon, if I pray enough, he'll be working again."

My father shut the door, and we drove off, got back on the street, crossed the bridge, and came into town. Right past the bridge, where we were supposed to turn right, my father kept on going straight. My mother wanted to know where he was going. He was going into town to buy us all an ice-cream cone.

Cota said she wanted vanilla and Maggie wanted chocolate and Frances wanted something with pecans and on it went, all of us putting our order in.

My grandmother reflected on her choice when we asked her what she was going to have. She finally decided on vanilla.

On the way home we went by the park, took a turn around it, and saw the men and women sitting on the benches cooling off. In front of the church we saw Father Zavala talking to some of the Mutualists who had just finished their meeting. He waved at us and we waved back. We were yelling his name. He yelled something back at us, and we didn't understand. This made us laugh.

"It's nice," my grandmother said looking out the window, "to go out once in awhile."

The Cotton Fiesta

The major cash crop of South Texas in those days was cotton. Every year there was a great celebration—the Cotton Fiesta—during August, the harvest season. The local gin had a contest rewarding the first bale of cotton that was brought in. The winning farmer received a modest cash prize and his picture appeared in the local weekly newspaper. My grandfather tried to win the Earliest Bale Contest one year by sharecropping a little acreage at the edge of town. He didn't win in spite of all the help he got from us.

The town went all out for the Cotton Fiesta. On the first Friday there would be an opening-day parade in the afternoon. The Cotton Fiesta Queen, who was crowned on the official opening day, would ride in an open car with the mayor, a little pudgy, hairless banker who spoke in rapid-fire bursts like an automatic weapon. The mayor insisted in giving all his speeches in horrible English. Apparently he was mayor for life. It was his job by default since no one else wanted the honor. The queen would be dressed in her long evening gown, waving at the sparse crowd. In the hot August sun, beads of perspiration would flow from the poor girl's forehead down her cheeks and from her elbows to her armpits as she elevated her arms to wave at the crowd. The mayor, beaming with pride, would wave with his hat in the opposite direction. When he wasn't waving, he was fanning himself with his hat. Driving them would be the young man who washed cars at the local car agency. Behind the mayor and the queen came the County Judge and his wife and children, also waving at us. All the other so-called dignitaries were there—city officials, county commissioners, the sheriff. The local FFA chapter had their float, usually with a sheep or a goat riding on a trailer eating grass. The Knights of Columbus was represented by two men dressed in plumed hats teetering on the back of a truck holding the mighty emblem of their order. One year, Maggie, the stoutest among us, was the Statue of Liberty on the Knights of Columbus float. She was dressed in a white sheet, a sash around her waist. Her job was to stand perfectly still while holding the fake torch. Naturally, we ran after the float, throwing anything we could find at her to make her move. Next came the San Diego Band and then the people on horseback. We loved the horses. It had always been our dream to ride a horse in the parade.

The Cotton Fiesta was the busiest during the four weekends in August. That was when the farmers came to town to buy groceries, clothes, and other supplies. The fiesta occupied an empty city lot that took the appearance of an old-world town plaza with all kinds of attractions around the perimeter and the people walking around and around inside its confines kicking up dust. Indeed, from afar one could spot the location of the fiesta by the cloud of dust suspended over the square block it occupied. More pronounced at night, the cloud of dust, illuminated by the many lights, was an eery sight. In the center of the grounds was a kiosk where the band played, the mayor gave his annual speech, and the queen was crowned. It was possible for a few couples, the ones who didn't care who stared at them, to dance in the kiosk. Around the kiosk were wooden benches where one could rest and enjoy the music after going around and around for so many hours. Here were found young couples anxious to talk to each other after a week of absence. Usually there was a chaperone or two with each girl—her sisters or cousins. Sometimes, depending on how modern the family was, there was none. The encounters led to innocent romantic moments, but with absolutely no physical displays of emotion. The attraction between the sexes was so great that on any night it was not unusual for a couple or two to get up from their seats, walk around the block a few times, mingle with the crowd, and then disappear between the many stands. They had run off to get married. The word would spread. By early the next morning, someone had come to our house to tell us the tales of the night before and inform my grandmother and my mother who had eloped. "The girl who lives with the Perez's, the one whose mother died when she was five and who was given to the Perez's."

"The real pretty one who works at the cleaners?"

"The same one."

"Who with?"

"She went off with the son of the carpenter Martinez."

"Which one? He has three."

"They say the one who works at the meat market."

"The middle one. He's too young to be getting married."

"You know how it is."

"I didn't know they went together."

"No one else did. They had been hiding their intentions for a long time it seems."

"And how is Justina taking it?"

"The girl's mother is crying, naturally."

People from all over the region rented spaces around the old square and set up their stands—tents, temporary wooden buildings and carnival games. Little food stands were set up where families could eat out in the open. There were some who made their entire living off the fiesta. The owner of the hobby horses who brought them out of storage by mid-July and cleaned and set them up for the children to ride was one. He kept the hobby horses going long after the Cotton Fiesta was over, well into November. Everyone in town could hear his music at night. The lady with the milk-bottle game was another. She kept on for a while longer, for as long as she could make money.

Smaller games of chance at the fiesta were the *manita*, similar to the wheel of fortune. It cost a penny a game to spin the fragile wooden stick with the celluloid tab at the end. Around and around it went, making a rat-a-tat noise as it slipped by the nails that separated the squares. The Boy Scouts ran the pitch-penny game, the squares so small the penny could hardly fit.

The *Lotería* was very popular with the older people. It was run by the church and by Father Zavala, of course. It attracted by far the largest crowds of all. On Friday, Saturday, and Sunday nights it was hard for the old women to find a place to sit. The *Lotería* is a Spanish form of bingo using a board with vertical columns filled with squares with both numbers and drawings, the drawings for the people who could not read. The people sat around the rectangle of long wooden benches under a tarp which protected them from the dust, each person with a card or two of the *lotería*. A table loaded with extra cards which Father Zavala had purchased in Spain stood in the center of the rectangle. Sitting at the table was a man who had been chosen for having a booming voice. He would turn the wire cage and pull out a few of the lettered balls. With his resonant voice, he would announce first the column, then the number and description of the figure.

"Fourth," he would yell out, giving the column. Then came the square, "forty-five, the Water Carrier." And the players would mark with a kernel of corn the drawing of the man laboring under the large water vat on his back.

On and on the caller would continue, placing each of the little balls into the round holes of his master board until a winner would scream out in delight. "*¡Buena!*" the winner would shout. Everyone applauded. It was time to gossip. Who had almost won? "I only lacked three to win," someone would say. "I missed by one," came a reply followed by a large contented sigh. It was the thrill of the night. The card was verified and the winner paid, the church keeping some of the money. The game cost, in those days, a nickel a card.

My grandmother and mother loved to play *lotería*. They so looked forward to it as they dressed and walked to the fiesta to sit down for the night to play. It was more of a ritual than anything else. It was a place to see old friends and gossip. The happenings of the town were aired every night. The most important news was who had died and the eternal problem of women—the latest unmarried girl who had become pregnant. Unmarried pregnancy was spoken of as a euphemism, meant to keep the younger children in the dark.

"*La engañó*," they would whisper, meaning, "He deceived her." We could never figure out how a man could make a young girl pregnant by deceiving her. "*Engañaron a la hija de Juanita*," they would murmur in between games of *lotería*. The word was passed on. Soon every one knew. Juanita, who was probably there playing *lotería*, knew, but she hid her pain and shame. It was easier to do when one knew sooner or later it would happen to someone else's daughter. And besides, the discomfort of the moment lasted a few months. Soon it would be time for the baby to come. Dr. Dunlap would deliver it and everyone would love it. The town made no distinctions about illegitimacy.

One of the greatest dangers of hanging around the Cotton Fiesta was being urinated on by the *frailecillo*, the blister beetle. These beetles were attracted to the lights and would swarm overhead, falling indiscriminately on people, letting out their caustic body fluid on the unsuspecting victim. The burning pain was considerable, and the blister took several hours to form. There was no antidote. If there had been one, we would have known. When the *frailecillo* urinated on you, that was it. You blistered painfully on that spot for several days.

Another potential catastrophe, in case you were well groomed and looking around for your favorite girl, was the *cinche del monte*, the stink beetle. If it let out its juices on your clothes or skin, it would make you stink forever and you had to walk downwind from the girls.

Despite the drawbacks, we loved the fiesta. Our biggest problem was not having money. The first night was particularly meaningful for us. We had a tradition. We would go sit behind Arzuaga's Hamburger Stand to smell the delicious aroma of ground meat cooking in its own grease. After we tired of that odor, we would go by Carrillo's Taco Place for the smell of tacos. At the hobby horses Juan, Matías, Cota, Maggie, and Frances would jump on the moving contraption, its waltz music blasting away, and act as though they were chaperoning the children who had paid for their rides. The operator, a man with glasses so thick they made his eyes look like a grasshopper's, would blow his whistle at them and jump onto the rotating platform trying to push them off.

Later, after we had walked a few miles going around and around the plaza, we would start to get hungry. Juan then would say that María Arzuaga, the hamburger lady, made her patties by pressing the meat inside her armpit, and that José, her husband, washed his feet in the same pan where he rinsed the lettuce and tomatoes. That would check our appetite for a while.

One summer, an Anglo carnival man rented a large lot and set up swings powered by a car engine. But no one rode the swings. While he was setting up his rig, we spread the false rumor through town that a young girl in nearby Benavides had been flung off those same swings the week before, that the girl, screaming, was seen catapulted through the air at a tremendous speed and altitude, and that the sheriff and a mounted posse had not found her in the dense brush yet, so dangerous the swings were. The old, scrawny man scratched his head, confused as the entire town went by ignoring him, his empty swings going wildly round and round, the engine backfiring once in a while to send puffs of nauseous exhaust throughout the crowd. Another failed carnival entrepreneur, an Anglo who thought he was going to rake in the money, brought over a Ferris wheel—an old, beat up rig which took him and a crew of two almost a week to set up. We would go see him and his crew work, making comments among ourselves. The rumor we started on the Ferris wheel was that the seats were unsafe. We had watched them set them up, and Matías thought we should warn the town. The rumor had it that the seats were more likely than not to flip completely around, dropping whomever was sitting on the highest point through the metal structure and down to the ground, a drop of some fifty or sixty feet. If the fall didn't kill you, then the blows the body took falling through the steel girders and cables would. You could be dead by the time you hit the ground. It had happened, Cota said, in San Antonio. She had read about it, but couldn't remember where. By the time the man and his crew of two finished setting up the Ferris wheel, we had convinced ourselves of its danger. After one week, the Ferris wheel man took the thing down and left town. He hated Mexicans, he was heard to say to his crew of two.

This year we were tired of not being part of the fiesta. We were tired of being on the sidelines watching everyone else have fun. We were tired of smelling the aroma of food. We wanted something more than our mother's and grandmother's cooking. We wanted desperately to buy something to eat. We needed work.

A few days before the parade, we walked to the edge of town where the milkman lived and begged him to lend us his old horse to ride in the parade. At first he would have nothing to do with us, but gradually we wore him down. He finally consented the day before the parade. We ran home and told our grandmother, and although somewhat skeptical, she relented when she realized the milkman had taken a greater chance on us than she would have.

On the morning of the parade, we got up early, got dressed, ate our breakfast, and could hardly wait for the hours to go by. The milkman promised to have the horse saddled and ready by one o'clock. This would give us plenty of time to get the horse to the parade, while We took turns riding it. We were there early and watched the milkman go into the pen, bridle the horse, and then saddle him. The horse turned around and looked at us. We felt humbled in the presence of such a large animal. Still we were determined. When the horse was ready, the milkman walked him out to the street and Juan immediately got on him. Matías had wanted to be first. He resented Juan getting up without asking if anyone wanted to be first.

Matías said, "You should always ask if anyone wants to be first."

"Why?" asked Juan, already on top of the horse and adjusting his feet on the stirrups.

"Because," said Cota, "it's not polite to just climb on a horse first without asking. Someone else might want to go first."

Juan said, "You wouldn't get on first?"

"No," said Matías and Cota.

"Well," Juan replied, "I saved you the trouble."

Matías was about to jump on the horse and knock Juan down when the milkman intervened. "I won't allow any fighting," he said. And with that he grabbed Sylvia and put her on the saddle behind Juan. "Two at a time," he said. "No more. The poor horse is old."

We began to count the steps the horse took, and after one hundred steps, we had to change riders. We must have changed places twenty or thirty times before we got to the start of the parade. The horse was pleasant enough, had a good walk and trot. He had been a milk horse for so long he would not go beyond a trot.

Our troubles came on the first turn on the parade route. Everyone turned left to get on the street that went through the center of town, but our horse, remembering his milk route, went right. We could not turn him to save ourselves. Finally, Juan and Matías, who were on the horse, got off and had to lead him by the bridle back to the street. At the street, we could see the parade getting further and further away. And then the horse would not budge. Nothing we could do would make him move. He stood more or less frozen in the middle of the street, confused from an experience far different from his daily routine. The band started playing, annoying him even more. The floats, although far in front, were still another distraction to him.

Frances was chosen to go get the milkman so that he would help us out. The milkman arrived with a smile on his face. "I should have known," he said. "Poor animal hasn't been ridden in twenty years. He only knows his route."

"Why didn't he misbehave before?" Matías wanted to know.

"Because you took him exactly on his route," the milkman explained. "It was when you tried to turn into town that he balked."

The milkman spoke to the horse, explained the situation to him as though the horse would understand. Surprisingly, the horse trusted him enough to follow him home.

"Well," Cota said as we all watched the milkman and the horse slowly fade away, "we didn't really want to be in the parade. I don't like for people to stare at me."

We did get a job that year at the knock-the-milk-bottle concession stand. Juan, Cota, Matías, Frances, Maggie and Sylvia ran the show, shouting out to the passersby to come and try their luck at knocking the milk bottles off the pedestal with three baseballs. Richard and I, as usual, got the dirty job. We had to run out and pick up the milk bottles, set them up, then scamper around looking for the balls. All this while some drunks continued with their game, whizzing the balls close to our heads.

With the job came an unexpected awakening. The stand owner, a frail little woman who smoked thin cigars and cursed every other word, made us swear, under threat of violence, that we would not tell anyone that the three bottles on the bottom row were loaded with about twenty pounds of lead. My brother and I practiced setting the heavy bottles on the bottom row, then the two lighter ones on top of those, followed by the single top bottle. Anyone could knock the top bottle down without much effort. The second row took some strength of impact, but the bottles would occasionally fall. The bottom row? No one could have ever knocked those bottles down and off the pedestal. It was embarrassing for us to see the bottom row get a solid hit and not budge a quarter of an inch, the ball ricocheting back to where it came. The prize for knocking all the bottles off the pedestal was an old teddy bear, faded and about ten years old.

We were paid a quarter, *dos reales*, each for working from six o'clock to past midnight, until no other drunk wanted to try his luck. When we arrived home, our mother and grandmother were waiting for us to scold us. Where had we been? They had worried for so long. They had arrived from the *lotería* at ten and had stayed up waiting for us.

The next night my brother Richard was running around looking for balls when he was hit on the back of the head with a baseball. Luckily the balls were soft, making it further impossible to knock the bottom bottles down. And, the drunk hadn't hit the ball very hard. It did hurt my brother though. He fell on impact, and I ran to him to see how he was. He had tears in his eyes and was dribbling from his nose. He did not cry. Other than that, he was all right. Juan, Matías, Maggie, and Cota got into an argument with the drunk over the incident, and the owner came over from her taco stand and fired all of us. She refused to pay us. We argued for some time, but she was adamant. We had ruined her business by being careless. No one else had gotten hit on the head before. She was blaming us. The anger stayed with us a few days.

Which was why we decided that on the official opening night, the second Saturday, when the mayor gave his speech followed by the crowning of the queen, we would let out a harmless black snake among the crowd around the kiosk.

We looked for and trapped the snake at the creek, keeping it alive in a shoe box with holes. On opening night, the mayor was sitting with several other men in the kiosk, looking pleasantly about him at the crowd of people gathered there. He couldn't quit smiling. He was so full of himself. The young queen was sitting by his side, her parents beside her. The band played a fanfare. The mayor got up to the microphone, adjusted it down to his size, and began to speak in his broken English of the beauty and pageantry of the Cotton Fiesta. "The winderfel peple of...ahem...this town..ahem...who makest it so. The sul of a towner," he reminded us, "was its spiritus of volun...tee...rismasum. Only peple mattersus," he said. On and on he went, telling us how beautiful we were. From behind, a drunk shouted for the mayor to sit down so the queen could be crowned. The mayor ignored him. He had the speech in him, and he was not going to let anyone stop him from delivering it. Finally, he was through. He looked back to the young girl. On cue, she stood up and the mayor took the old, faded crown out of its box. As he went over to the queen, the crown raised to place it over her head, Juan let out the snake from inside his shirt and yelled at the same time.

The crowd screamed so loud that the sound was picked up by the microphone and carried throughout the fiesta. The *lotería* was suspended. Juan had yelled out, "Alicante!", the dreaded hoop snake found only in South Texas. It coils into a hoop and travels faster than any human, whipping everyone in its path. To say that the crowd vanished for half an hour is stopping short. The *lotería* came to a complete halt, something never before seen. The old women climbed up on the benches to scream. María Arzuaga ran, leaving the hamburgers to burn. The hobby horses were vacated in a rush of parents trying to protect their children. A drunk threw a baseball erratically, hitting the mean owner in the back of her head. The mayor, who had torn out of the kiosk like a hurricane, was half a block away when he decided his little heart could not support him. He fell to the ground clutching his chest. Later, we heard he was bedridden for some time.

We never got to eat a hamburger at the Cotton Fiesta. It was one of those things that, being unattainable, one tends to let pass. We had so much more important things to do.

We spent some of that year putting dust into used cotton sacks of Bull Durham Tobacco. Under the cover of darkness we would hide behind the parked cars and loosen the draw strings on the sacks before we threw them over the *loterí,* watching the dust empty out of the sacks as they sailed over the tarp, the dust settling on the players. We sat close to the hamburger stand, staring at people, trying to see if we could mesmerize them into dropping their hamburgers. And the rest of the time we spent hanging around the milk bottle stand, telling everyone that the bottom milk bottles were so heavy not even Superman could knock them off.

Reviving a Hen

In those days there was an abundance of birds in South Texas. We knew the Spanish name for the birds, but little else. And even at that, we were not very good, often not knowing which bird was which, arguing among ourselves about the names of the birds.

My Uncle Mercé, the lunatic, knew more about birds than anyone else in town. He knew how they flew, where they nested and how they built their nests. He could even identify the different birds' nests. There was the killdeer, which we trapped with a wooden box and corn for bait. We called him the *tildío*, a latinized version of the English name. Although we seldom caught the bird, when we did we didn't know what to do with him. He was horrible to eat; he tasted like epsom salts. The crow was fascinating. We could follow the crow for hours, watching him push everybody around, stealing food. The whippoorwill was noisy. The wren was the most prolific, but horrible to eat also. The cardinal was the most beautiful. The scissortail was the oddest in the way it flew.

We would go to the creek to spend whole days running after birds, trying to shoot them down with our little sling-shots made from forks of mesquite and strips of old inner tubes. For a pouch, we cut the tongue off an old shoe and tied it between the ends of the two rubber strips. In the pouch we would place the stone used as ammunition.

One time we cut the tongues off an old pair of shoes we found in the shed and then found out they belonged to an uncle who was storing his clothes there. He had a fit when he discovered the shoes without tongues. No one admitted anything, although my grandmother conducted a mini-investigation.

My Uncle Mercé had told us that to revive a bird, all you had to do was raise the tail feathers, place your lips about an inch from the hole, and blow air up its rear-end.

As soon as someone was lucky enough to stun a bird, we would run to it, pick it up, and begin to blow into its rear-end. But it never seemed to work for us.

At least once, we had prayed it would work.

We had been messing around the yard, throwing things at each other, playing at first, but then getting more serious after Matías hit Cota very hard with a rock. Then we started throwing rocks at Matías. Matías was picking up the rocks thrown at him and throwing them back at us. He threw a rock and hit my sister Sylvia, and she began to cry. The juices of anger were stirred when the defenseless Sylvia was hurt. We took off after Matías, and Matías took off running. He ran across the street into *Tía* Chata's yard.

Tía Chata was a very large, fat lady. Her arms were almost as thick as my waist was then. She was beautiful and kind, always in wonderful spirits. When she played the piano, her style was to attack the instrument, making it almost bounce off the floor. All she knew were marches and waltzes, and she played both with equal passion. You could swear the house was shaking when she sat at the piano every afternoon. She lived across the street from us and almost directly across from the rectory.

Tía Chata's yard was huge, a quarter of a city block. Her house was big by our standards and made of formed limestone blocks called *sillares*. Each block was about a cubic yard in size. The blocks had been raised and put in place using mules that pulled ropes over winches and pulleys. It was a common form of construction in the days of the early settlers. The roof was made of long, wide tin strips. Her house was always cool in the summer, its windows large, reaching almost from floor to ceiling all around the concrete porch which surrounded the house.

Tía Chata was a spinster who had raised her dead sister's four sons from very early childhood, and had done a splendid job of raising them, too. She was one of those ladies who went to the Rosary every night along with my grandmother. Her hobbies were raising canaries, which she kept caged inside double-screened windows. Passing by her house, one could hear them singing all day long, Chata, singing along with them. In the afternoon, when Chata sat at the piano to play, the canaries would hover against the limestone walls wondering about the significance of the torrent of noise. At night she would cover her precious canaries with sheets to allow them to sleep.

Her other hobby was raising chickens for eggs for the family. She worked out in the yard most of the day, doing something or other. She was never idle. She was also always studying something new. She spoke no English at all, but very proper Spanish. She had no qualms about correcting what we said, making sure we used the right word.

Once she asked me how old I was, and when I told her, she calculated that it was all right for me to do her the favor of climbing up the windmill to untangle the cable on the brake. I climbed nervously. It was a beautiful sight from the top of the windmill. *Tía* Chata cautioned me to be careful. She was afraid I would fall. Juan, Matías, Cota, Maggie, Frances, Richard, and Sylvia were egging me on. "If you should hurt yourself, I would never forgive myself," she yelled up to me. "Not to mention what your grandmother and mother would do to me." Then she laughed out loud. I could see the whole town. Across the street I could see Walter Meek's windmill at my same level. Before coming down, I stood up and beat my chest and screamed like Tarzan. By the time I reached the ground, *Tía* Chata was laughing her jolly laugh. She put her hand inside her apron pocket and pulled out a coin and gave it to me...a nickel.

Tía Chata's favorite hen and her biggest layer was one she called *La Blanca*. This hen laid at least one egg a day, sometimes two. *Tía* Chata loved her, treated her with the same affection she had for everyone else. She spoke to her out in the yard as if she were a person. She told the hen her problems, her joys. Every morning the routine was the same. *Tía* Chata would come out before breakfast with a pail of chicken feed, call up her chickens, *La Blanca* proudly waggling ahead of the pack, knowing she was the preferred one. *Tía* Chata would talk to all of them, but *La Blanca* got the most attention. *Tía* Chata scattered more feed in front of her than anyone else. *Tía* Chata had had her for several years now, and she would often tell the story of how she had raised her from an egg. Their bond was such that if *Tía* Chata was in the yard, the hen was not far behind.

Every morning *Tía* Chata would gather the eggs from the little hen house in which she locked her chickens at night.

This morning, *Tía* Chata was outside hand-watering her bougainvilleas. She turned around to see what we were doing.

Matías had run half-way through the yard and we were getting closer. Matías had made a turn to evade us and was running toward the windmill. He managed to dodge us while still going for the windmill. He went around the windmill and was running back from where he came. We ran around the windmill after him. Finally, he ran toward Chata, hoping this would make us stop.

We saw the look of confusion on *Tía* Chata's face. She did not know what to make of all this running and screaming. I was behind the pack. I knew I could never catch Matías, so I picked up a rock and threw it at him as hard as I could. I had no hope of reaching him with the rock. The rock took off from my hand and sailed more to the right than I had meant. I watched it go off in that direction. The rest of the pack stopped when they saw the rock overhead. Matías stopped to see why we weren't chasing him. The rock continued on its way, reached the top of its arc, and then began to descend. Slowly, painfully, I watched along with the others as the rock came down toward *La Blanca,* who was close by *Tía* Chata, busily pecking away at some bug on the ground. The rock could not have been thrown more perfectly if one had wanted to kill the most favored chicken. But then, as the rock glided down, I thought that even if I did hit the chicken I would not hurt it in any way. I was too little to cause much damage.

But providence being what it is, the rock hit the chicken on the only place where it could kill it. The rock hit *La Blanca* on top of the head. What could one say to *Tía* Chata to soothe her feelings? She had been following the rock as we all had. When it hit the chicken on top of the head, the hen flopped over dead. *Tía* Chata let out a scream. The hen experienced several muscular twitches and a few gapes of the beak. Death was instantaneous. By the time *Tía* Chata rushed the few steps to reach *La Blanca,* the chicken was dead.

Quickly we ran to *La Blanca. Tía* Chata had her in her arms, crying. Juan took her away from *Tía* Chata. He began to blow air up its rear-end. Then Cota tried it. Frances kept

on. Then Maggie. Matías had returned and tried it also. At
last it came my turn. Cota was holding the limp chicken, the
rear-end in my face, looking at me like she knew I was in a
lot of trouble. I had to revive the hen. Frantically, I held the
tail up and blew and blew. I'm sure my face was red with
fear, embarrassment, hyperventilation. I was light-headed. I
staggered around. *Tía* Chata finally could not take any more
of this. She began to laugh. She could not figure out what it
was we were doing. She had never seen this form of resusci-
tation before.

She went in her house and everything was quiet for a
while. We sat on the porch, passing the dead chicken around,
each one trying to revive her. Then we heard *Tía* Chata begin
to pound on the piano—first a march, *Zacatecas*, then a very
sad waltz, *Morir Soñando*. We persisted in trying to revive
the chicken, but our efforts had become half-hearted. The
canaries were screaming.

When she came out, we could tell she had been crying. I
told her how sorry I was, and she gave me a smile, reached
out for me, and engulfed me with her enormous body in a
hug.

"I know you didn't mean it," she said. "It was an acci-
dent." Then she asked the inevitable question: "Who in the
world taught you children to blow into a chicken's rear-end to
revive it?"

"Mercé," we said.

She had the courtesy not to laugh again. She asked us if
we would bury *La Blanca* for her. She did not want to eat
her. She went in to keep on with the piano.

We didn't bury the hen. We dug a hole behind *Tía* Chata's
house, threw a rock in, and covered it. Juan stuck the chicken
inside his pants and we took it to the creek. There, we
plucked it and started a fire and roasted it. But *La Blanca*
was so hard and tough we couldn't cut her up to eat. We tried
boiling her. After an hour, we couldn't eat her. We boiled her
some more. In all we must have boiled the hen two or three
hours. It took that long before we could eat her. And then she
was not so tender. She was the toughest bird we ever ate, and
by now she tasted like killdeer.

Chata did tell my grandmother and mother, and we were
forbidden to ever go into her yard again. But Chata inter-

vened. She forgave us and she told my grandmother and mother we could play in her yard.

We were allowed to play in *Tía* Chata's yard on one condition. "If you kill another one of her hens, then I'm going to whip all of you," my grandmother warned us.

There was another side to *Tía* Chata we had never known, a playful, sadistic side. Although she forgave us, she never quite let us forget we had killed her dear hen. When she called me to climb up the windmill to fix the cable on the brake, she would remind me of what I had done. Then she would reach inside her apron pocket and give me a nickel.

And afterwards, when we would go past her house and she would be out in the yard or cooling herself off, seated at the porch, she would say, "There go the beautiful children who killed my beloved *La Blanca*. How I miss her." She would sigh. Her guilt-inducing sadness was temporary though. Soon, she would give out her robust laugh and then ask, "Which of you is the most beautiful?"

"Matías," Juan would answer.

"Juan," Matías would answer.

"Cota," Maggie would answer.

"Maggie," Frances would answer.

And so on.

Then she would fan her face, red from the heat of the day, and tilt her head to listen to her beloved canaries. "I'll never have a hen like her again," she would say. "Never. Not even if I live to be a hundred years old."

At the end of the block we could hear the thunder coming from her house, the introduction to the march *Zacatecas*.

We were never able to steal enough hens from the creek to replace *La Blanca*. *Tía* Chata refused them all. She knew we had stolen them and she was much too honest to accept them. And besides, her hen was irreplaceable.

She died many years later, still asking my mother how the hen-killer was doing.

The Town Dog

The town dog could tell what day it was. It bothered us that this dog was so smart. Besides knowing what day it was, he knew that there was a fine line between the dignity of a beggar and the repugnance of a parasite.

Late Sunday afternoons, he would show up across the street at *Tía* Chata's and sleep on the cool concrete porch. He would spend the night there, and morning would find him still lying on his side, breathing regularly with not a care in the world. Never would the mongrel move out of the way for the poor woman. It was she who had to respect him and his territory. He'd stretch out, yawn, scratch off some fleas, and then wait for *Tía* Chata to feed him the scraps left over from breakfast. He'd watch through the window at *Tía* Chata getting ready for early Mass. When she came out, he would escort her to the steps of the church as though she could never find her own way without him. He'd wait patiently outside for the Mass to be over. When the women came out, he would sit up attentively, looking for *Tía* Chata. He would then spot her, walk over, and lick her hand. He would accompany her back home and spend the rest of the day sleeping or patrolling her yard, chasing away any other dogs who might be a threat to *Tía* Chata's hens. Sometime during the day, he never failed to prance around as though he owned the yard and was earning his keep. He paid particular attention not to offend *Tía* Chata by disturbing the canaries. He walked around the canaries on tip-toes.

Monday evenings he would trot off across the street to stay with Father Zavala on the rectory steps. Father Zavala didn't mind him. He stepped over the lying dog as he went in or out of the rectory. On Tuesday morning the dog was fed

breakfast leftovers by Otilia, who cooked for Father Zavala.
At the sound of the bells, he would walk over to the front of
the church and go through the ritual of smelling everyone
who entered the church for early Mass. Tuesday was more of
a day of leisure for him than for Father Zavala. He would
sleep all day, opening an eye once in a while, not having to
protect any hens, letting out a bored sigh as though he were
doing the priest a favor by being there. Then when he had the
priest's attention, he would take on a sad countenance as if to
tell him how tiresome this holy life could be.

Tuesday night you could find him at the center of town, at
the intersection where the drug store, the Post Office, the old
movie house, and the barbershop were located. He'd sleep
there, moving alternatively from one place to the other
depending on how much the noise in any particular place
interfered with his trying to fall asleep. In the morning, he
would walk by the San Diego Cafe and get a bite to eat at the
rear where the cook had thrown out some old food. He would
spend Wednesday in town, going from store to store acting like
he was going to buy something and then backing off as though
someone had insulted him and made him change his mind.

Wednesday night he would spend at the top of the courthouse steps. In the morning, he would follow the county
employees around the hallways. Sometimes he would take in
a trial or two if he had the time and if he felt the trial was
well-attended. He loved a grand entrance into the courtroom.
He reserved some time to visit the prisoners in jail, licking
their hands and trying to cheer them up. It was up to the people there to feed him whatever they had left of their lunch.
Usually the jailer had some food that the prisoners wouldn't
eat, and the dog got to eat it. Naturally, he was sure to be at
the jail at mealtimes.

Thursday he would come to sleep with us. He enjoyed
spring and summer, the hottest time of the year in South
Texas, since we often slept outside on the porch and he could
sleep among us, spreading his fleas around. Bright and early
on Friday mornings, he would start to bark to get us out of
bed. He was ready to play. He ate whatever we could give
him, but it didn't matter to him. He wanted to play. He'd run
to the creek with us and spend most of the time in the cave.
Sometimes he would be allowed to play baseball with us. He
was perfect at chasing down the batter.

Friday, early in the evening, he would leave for the COD Bar downtown. He knew where the action was on that night. He'd sleep on the low steps, watching all the men go in and out. He'd spend Saturday at the bar, looking around, getting up once in a while when someone would call him, taking a bite of food here and there.

Saturday night, he would disappear and we would not see him again until Sunday night when he would show up at *Tía* Chata's.

He knew Sunday was a day of rest.

We followed him and found out where he lived when he wasn't in town. He lived at the creek in the center of a heavily wooded area. He had a hole dug out in a clearing from which he could see anyone approaching. This is where he stayed on Saturday night and most of the day Sunday, resting. From his home atop the creek bank he could see the little town, see all the goings-on Saturday night and most of Sunday.

He would not deviate from this routine. Somehow he knew what day of the week it was from his observations of the townspeople.

We decided to trick the dog, to see if we could confuse him. On a Friday morning, when he was outside barking for us to come out and play, we ran to the creek with him and took him inside our cave. Juan had brought food for him and Matías had brought a pail for water. We left food and water for him and sealed the cave. He spent all of Friday and Saturday in the cave without sunlight. We could hear him snoring inside. Nothing seemed to bother him. We fed him and gave him water again, and late Sunday evening we turned him loose. We were watching him to see what he would do. He came out of the cave and acted disoriented for a while. He stretched his limbs and looked out to the town spread out below him. His little eyes focused on several points. We ran back and he ran back with us. We thought we had him fooled. He was going back home with us. We were laughing at him, and he seemed to enjoy the run, having been cooped up for such a long time. We were egging him on to follow us. He was in the middle of the pack, running, his tongue hanging out. At the corner before we got home, he began to veer to his left. We tried to get him to go straight ahead with us, but he was determined, and the lure of his senses too strong. He pushed his way out of the pack and headed straight for *Tía* Chata's with us running after him. At *Tía* Chata's, he barked for her just to tell her he had arrived and would be needing something to eat in the morning.

He knew it was Sunday evening and that *Tía* Chata would be waiting for him.

Later on, with nothing else to do, we tried to confuse him again and again. We blindfolded him once and took him across town away from the creek. On the day he spent with us, we acted as if it were Sunday and we were going to Mass. The next week when he came by, we hid from him and watched his reaction. He slept on our porch as though he knew exactly where we were. In time, we put him in a pillow case and made him spend all day at the movies with us. Nothing worked. There was something he was aware of that we could not discover.

Some people said the dog had magical powers, that he could cast the evil eye. But my grandfather said it wasn't true.

"No animal, except man, has ever tried to hurt another with witchcraft. All dogs are very observant," my grandfather said. "Why, a dog is smart enough to create his own fleas."

"Why would a dog want to have fleas?" we asked.

"To keep himself occupied," my grandfather replied.

My grandfather was right. We knew the dog was very observant. We could see him looking about the town from his vantage point. It was a combination of the town's activities, its routine, that led the dog along certain paths, made him come to the right conclusions. It may have been the ringing of the bell, the wailing of the town siren, the music coming from the center of town, the visions of the old women dressed in black and weaving their way to the rosary at different times during the week, the daily movements of Father Zavala, of the town mayor, the tradesmen in town, the different smells coming from the kitchens, the variations in the sounds of conversations, the activity at the courthouse, the gathering of people on Saturdays at the barbershop, Chata's pounding on the piano.

Whatever it was, the dog had it figured out even if we never could. As for us children, we had to finally admit that lowly mongrel was the one creature in town we could never fool.

The Raffle

We were at the courthouse one day taking in a trial as we enjoyed doing from time to time. We used to sit in the narrow balcony, watching the proceedings from above. On those occasions, Matías enjoyed acting like a lawyer. He would interrogate us about anything that had happened around the house. Who had eaten the last tortilla? He was relentless at times, looking for evidence in the kitchen. Once he convicted his brother Juan by matching the teeth marks on a tortilla against Juan's bite. When he got into those moods, there was nothing we could get away with. He was prosecutor, judge, and jury all in one.

This time a man had been accused of killing another man during an argument. The case was interesting, and the courtroom was air-conditioned. It was nice to get out of the hot sun.

We knew the accused man. He lived not four blocks away from our house. He was testifying that day. The prosecuting attorney claimed the man had lost his temper when a neighbor's dog entered his backyard and bothered him. The neighbor came out and argued with the man over the dog. It was nothing at first, but the argument got heated and the accused asked the neighbor to please stay put while he went and got his rifle. The victim was not about to run. His pride had him believing he could stop a bullet. He calmly stood his ground while the accused went inside, loaded the rifle, and came out with the rifle in his hands. The victim dared the man to shoot him. The man obliged and shot him once in the chest and then walked over and shot him again. The facts of the trial were so petty they were hard to believe. Both the victim's and the defendant's families were there looking with hate at each

94

other. We were thinking they might have a fight right inside the courtroom.

During a recess, we were wandering around the hallways when a man who knew our father and grandfather came out of the tax office and greeted us. He had information for both our father and grandfather. We were sorry, but our father worked all day six days a week, and he had no time to listen to any gossip from the courthouse. And our grandfather was back in San Antonio, working nights at another liquor store on East Commerce. My grandmother worried about him at his age, staying up all night at the liquor store. He had sold the truck without doors and had bought an old used car. He wouldn't be driving in until Friday night late, and he would stay until noon Sunday when he would leave back for work.

The man was disappointed to hear our story. He looked like he would burst if he didn't regurgitate this gossip on someone. He was so anxious, he decided we were good enough to hear the news. The gossip around the courthouse was exciting. George B. Parr owned a Shetland pony and was going to raffle it at the courthouse. Our father and grandfather would probably like to know. Maybe they would want to buy a ticket for the raffle.

What luck we had! What we thought would be boring gossip had become a dream come true. We could have our own horse, at last. We could ride in the Cotton Fiesta parade, taking turns.

The gentleman giving us the news, whom we knew as *El Tuerto*, or the One-Eyed, was as delighted as we were. He had children, and he was going to buy the first ticket for the raffle as soon as all the arrangements were completed. We could see his one eye moving around on his face like a large floating brown marble.

Forget about the trial. We ran home to tell my grandmother and my mother about the Shetland pony. They were against it. Where would we put him? Did we realize how much trouble a horse created? We would not change our minds. We would try for the pony no matter what. Finally, to quiet us down, my grandmother said we would wait for my grandfather to return. The decision would be up to him.

The town was getting worked up over the raffle during the week. The trial, which had been so important some days before, was forgotten. The man was found guilty to a courtroom almost empty, except for the town dog and the victim's family. The dog got up after the verdict came in and went and licked the defendant's hand, bidding him goodbye for the five years he was to be gone. The victim's family promised to kill him when he returned to town. The dog accompanied the condemned to jail, made sure he was properly locked up, and then stayed around for table scraps.

All of a sudden, everyone knew about the Shetland pony. George B. Parr's daughter had never ridden it. The pony was a nuisance to him, so he had decided to raffle it and donate the money to Father Zavala and the church.

Friday night we were waiting anxiously for my grandfather to drive in from San Antonio. He was late, and we could hardly stand it. When he did not show after an hour, we decided to run to the courthouse to sit on the curb and watch for the car to come down the highway. We waited another hour until we saw the little desolate lights from the car approaching. We knew it was him. He always drove so slowly and way off to the right side of the road. We could see the car cautiously weave on and off of the shoulder. If we hadn't been waiting to beg from him, we would have been angry to see him. Slowly he approached, his lights dimming and then becoming brighter. He must have had trouble with them on the trip.

When he turned off the highway and into the street, we stood up, ready to run to the car. He saw us and honked. We ran beside the car. Juan and Matías ran fast enough to jump on the running board. They were telling him about the raffle. He could not understand, the noise of the car making it difficult for him. By now they were screaming. He was leaving the rest of us behind. We were catching the exhaust fumes.

When he turned into the driveway, we were a half block away. Juan and Matías were bending his ear.

"Wait...wait," he said. "Let me get out of the car. What nonsense do you children have up your sleeves now?"

"No nonsense," said Juan. "There's going to be a raffle. A Shetland pony. The raffle is going to be at the courthouse next Saturday."

"And what about it?" my grandfather asked, teasing us. He had opened the car door and was easing himself out. "What do I have to do with the raffle?"

"We've got to buy a ticket," Cota pleaded.

He let us go on, each of us begging him. If we had the pony we would take care of it. We promised. We had figured everything out during the week. Each day one of us would be responsible for the pony. We would clean him, brush him, feed him, water him. We could build a pen with the boards left from the old shed my grandfather and father had torn down after my grandmother sold the goats. We would dig the posts and nail the boards. All our grandfather had to do was buy the ticket.

The next day, we all went with my grandfather to the courthouse. The courthouse was packed with people. It was a disappointment to us. We had figured that the fewer the number of people who knew about the raffle, the better our chances. My grandfather stood in line while we played on the grass outside. Slowly he moved up the line until he was inside the tax collector's office and we couldn't see him.

In a short while he came out smiling. He had been able to afford the ticket, and he had it in his hand. We were full of excitement walking back to the house. He would let each of us hold the ticket. We would read it, would read the number over and over again. We would memorize the number, and then pray it would be the first one chosen. My brother was acting like a horse, making whinnying noises. I was running around my grandfather, bucking like a horse. Matías was riding Juan's back, acting as though he were on a horse. The girls were running back and forth with so much abandon that my grandfather had to get after them. We were going to have a pony.

We started off full of love and respect. Juan was being very nice to all of us, especially Matías. Cota was being very nice and caring. Maggie, and Frances likewise. My sister Sylvia and brother Richard and I were the best of friends.

Saturday night we had gotten together to talk about ways to make sure we won the raffle. Matías came up with an idea we all thought would work. Matías' plan called for all of us to get up very early on Sunday to get to the sacristy before Father Zavala. It would be easy to get into the sacristy since my brother Richard and I were to help Father Zavala with the early Mass. We would take the ticket to the altar and place it there without Father Zavala knowing about it. He would bless the ticket three times, once during each Mass, when he blessed the altar with the incense.

We got up earlier than usual, without explaining to my grandmother why all of a sudden we had to go to the early Mass and left her wondering what we were up to. We sneaked into the sacristy while Matías made sure Father Zavala was not watching. The church was deserted. We got on the altar and Juan, Cota, Maggie and Frances tipped the statue of Jesus Christ while Matías slid the ticket under His bare feet. We straightened out the altar and went back into the sacristy. My brother and I stayed behind, and the rest went back around to enter the church through the front door. Father Zavala arrived in a hurry. When we went with him to help ring the first bell for the Mass, he saw Juan, Matías, Cota, Frances, Maggie, and Sylvia seated in a pew. He looked around and saw no one else. We could see his mind straining. He had never seen us all there for an early Mass. He decided to let matters be rather than try to find out what we were doing.

That Sunday he blessed our raffle ticket three times. In the afternoon, while Father Zavala took his afternoon nap, we were back at church retrieving the ticket. Without realizing it, he had given us the upper hand.

Then it started. On Monday Juan wanted it known that he would be the first one to ride the pony. Everyone else objected and we started to argue, each one pleading for the chance to be first. Juan wanted to saddle the horse all the time, since he was the strongest and could tighten the cinch tighter than anyone else.

"We don't want the saddle slipping off to one side," he explained.

Matías claimed to be stronger and he challenged Juan to a wrestling match. They both had a go of it for an hour, until they could hardly stand up.

Cota wanted to bridle the pony and Maggie got angry. Sylvia wanted to feed it an apple a day. No one wanted that. If we had apples, we would eat them ourselves. Sylvia wanted to cry. My brother Richard wanted to mount the pony from the right side and all of us made fun of him. He was going to get killed. Juan wanted to name the horse, and no one would let him. He would shout the name above everyone else shouting to drown him out. Cota said she knew how to train the horse to shake hands, and we argued about making the horse do something so silly. After all, it was not a dog. That remark inspired Frances to say that maybe the pony could sleep in the house. She was booed down immediately.

By the middle of the week, none of us were talking to each other. We had not agreed on a single thing. We did reconcile when we were told the pony would be shown at the courthouse lawn on Thursday. We went together, but not in a very friendly mood.

We could see the pony from afar, the people close to him, trying to pet him. The horse was brown and white with very short hair. He had the most beautiful face we had ever seen on a horse, nothing like the milkman's horse. His nose was straight and not dished out. The curvature of his mouth and his lips were a perfect compliment to his large muscular jaw. He took to the bridle easily. His eyes were huge and shining, giving him the look of intelligence. His ears were propped and always on the move, picking up sounds all around him. He was perky like most Shetland ponies. He would turn around quickly and strike out if he felt intimidated. But we felt we could correct this bad habit. One day with us and he wouldn't strike out or bite. He would love us too much. His little hooves had been painted black. He had his saddle, which we saw up close. It was the most beautiful saddle we had ever seen—a child's saddle, gleaming with silver studs, a rich maroon shade, with covers on the stirrups. The bridle was silver-studded and the reins were long and had designs embossed on them. We were standing next to him, admiring him. What a beautiful addition he would make to our family. All our resentments, our arguments, dissolved for a precious few moments. We were all one family then. What a thrill it would be to win. And with our blessed ticket, who could stop us? I looked around and all of us were grinning.

But then Juan tried to stroke the pony. Matías would not allow him, nor would Cota nor Maggie nor Frances. They were afraid the pony would bond with Juan. Juan sneaked around them and stroked the pony's nose. Matías shoved Juan out of the way. The pony reared and kicked. Juan shoved Matías back and they got into a fight in no time. Matías and Juan were rolling on the ground, wrestling in the dust. The pony was spooked. He was trying to tear away from his halter rope. Luckily, he was tied to a large spike in the ground. A small crowd of people gathered to see the fight. Cota took this opportunity to shout that the name of the pony

would be Hiyo Silver, after the Lone Ranger's horse. Frances
wanted to name it Lassie. Juan and Matías were locked into
one human form, neither giving in, neither able to move the
other one. Arguments erupted from all sides. No one could
name the pony. Maggie said the pony already had a name
and to change it would confuse it. By this time Juan and
Matías were running out in front of us, exchanging words of
battle. I wanted to feed the pony. Everyone said I was too
small to do anything but ride in back with someone else. I
was deeply hurt. I had wanted to do tricks on the pony like
the Cisco Kid. I had named the pony Blaze, but had not had
the courage to tell anyone.

The arguing continued without stopping Thursday and
Friday until my grandmother said she was going to tell my
grandfather about us. Then she was going to tear the ticket
and throw it away. That shut us up.

Friday night we waited angrily for my grandfather. We
were sitting on the curb at the courthouse. We knew it was
him when we saw the lights dimming as he hit a bump. He
had not fixed the lights. He kept forgetting since he never
drove the car at night in San Antonio. We ran home behind
the car. Juan and Matías were on the running board. We
were being careful not to offend each other.

My grandmother noticed how well we were behaving and
did not mention to my grandfather anything about our arguments.

"How have you behaved?" he asked us all as he sat to eat.

We could not have been more pleasant to each other. Cota
told him about going to see the pony on Thursday. It was
beautiful. Brown and white with short hair, like a toy. Now
everyone wanted to speak at the same time. We told him
about the saddle, the most beautiful saddle we had ever seen.
No one mentioned the fight.

"How much does a saddle like that cost?" we asked him.

"A lot," he said, and we knew he was right. My grandfather knew a little about everything.

We were so happy to have my grandfather back. With
him around there would be no arguments. He would decide
who would ride first. How to mount the horse. What its name
would be. Whether it should eat apples or not. Whether it
could sleep inside or not. Who would feed it and when and
how much. Who would water it and when and how much.

What it would eat. He had to have a proper diet. I asked him if we should wear our old boots when we rode it, and he reflected for a time and said we should.

"Boots," he said, finishing his meal, "are meant for riding horses. That's why they're pointed at the tip. So that the foot doesn't get caught in the stirrup and the rider does not get dragged on the ground should he fall."

How exciting that was. We would all wear boots.

"No riding barefooted," he said. "If I catch anyone riding barefooted, then they have to get off and not ride for a week."

What a disaster that would be, not to ride Blaze for a week. I knew I could feed him and my grandfather agreed.

He said, "You let him feed the pony when its his turn. And if he needs help, then I want all of you to help him."

I was being much loved that night. Everyone volunteered to help me feed Blaze. I felt bold with all the help I was getting. I said, "His name is Blaze."

There was a silence in the kitchen.

"I like the name," my grandfather said, agreeing with me.

The name Blaze was all right according to all the rest of the gang, although I could see the resentment in Juan and Matías and Cota and Maggie. I had beaten them to naming the horse.

"Then Blaze it will be," my grandfather said. "Now to bed with all of you. We need to be at the courthouse early in the morning. We want to get there so we can sit up front."

We decided to sleep outside on the porch, and we could hardly sleep. Not only were we very excited, the arguments about Blaze seemed to go on and on. I finally dozed off after being told the pony's name was not to be Blaze. Blaze was a sissy name, and this was a horse and not a mare. I was only able to come to a shallow slumber, what with all the words being spoken. Now the saddle belonged to Matías and the pony to Juan. Frances was up, hitting Juan for owning the pony and not wanting to share. Matías said he could sell the saddle and buy a horse and a saddle with the money. The saddle wouldn't be as nice, but at least he wouldn't have to share with anyone. Juan argued that he could sell the pony and buy a horse and a saddle, too. He would have a lesser horse and saddle, but he wouldn't let Matías, Cota, Maggie, Frances, anyone, ride his horse. I don't remember anything after that, but in the morning when I awoke, the sheets and covers were thrown all over the porch. I must have slept through some fight.

We ate breakfast quietly with my grandfather. We did not want to jeopardize our chances with him. My grandmother said nothing about the sheets and covers on the porch. Afterwards, we walked to the courthouse.

We could see several cars parked around the courthouse square. We were a little early, and my grandfather was satisfied we could get to sit up front. When we got into the tax office, several families had beaten us to the front row so we took the chairs right behind them. Soon the crowd grew larger, and by eight o'clock the big room was full. The mayor arrived and sat up front at a small table, but not before trying to greet everyone there. Father Zavala came in right after the mayor and took his seat by the mayor. He had in his hands the box full of raffle tickets. He placed the box on the table between himself and the mayor. He saw us and winked. I thought it could be a signal and told my brother. My brother said I was crazy. Father Zavala was not about to help anyone cheat on a raffle. Still more people arrived. There were families out in the hallway. The mayor could not sit still. Every once in a while he would get up to greet the new arrivals.

At nine o'clock, the mayor got up and said a few words about the town and how proud he was to represent it. As usual, he tried to speak in English and did a bad job of it. He spoke of the spirit of "coparatation." Then he spoke in a mixture of English and Spanish and no one could understand him. Someone out in the hallway asked what was going on, and then we heard the low murmurings of explanation and then loud laughter. The mayor then stuck to Spanish in order to be understood. The crowd applauded.

Then came the good part—the raffle. The mayor explained the process of a reverse raffle. It would not be the first name drawn that would win. The winner would be the last name drawn. The news caught everyone by surprise. When had the rules been changed?

"This morning," the mayor replied. "It's only fair. And it adds a lot of drama to the event."

We stood to protest and my grandfather made us sit down. It wasn't fair. We had prayed all week to be the first name drawn. Father Zavala had blessed the ticket at three Masses so it would be chosen first. If we had known, we would have prayed to be the last name drawn. What a time for the mayor to confuse God. We lost all hope. We might as well leave, we told my grandfather. He made us sit down once again. Some of the parents were very angry by the time word reached the back of the room and the hallways. We agreed with them and could not believe my grandfather would go along.

Father Zavala stood to quiet the crowd. He had agreed to the format. The crowd accepted the decision, but not without some bitter words. Quickly, before more turmoil could erupt, the mayor glanced at Father Zavala. Father Zavala stood and went to the box full of tickets and began to shake it. By now the crowd was so mesmerized with the raffle that they forgot about the mayor's format. Father Zavala reached inside the box and pulled out a ticket. He read the number. It wasn't us! We heard a moan from both parents and children. It was *El Tuerto*, the one-eyed man. He had been the first to buy a ticket and the first to lose. He and his family got up dejected and threaded their way out through the crowd. The children were crying. We were smiling. The next number came out of box and another moan filled the room with disappointment. A couple and two children left the room amid cries. Another number. Not us. More people left. God must not have heard our prayers. Or maybe He knew the mayor had changed the rules. Whatever it was, it was working. We were smiling broadly. Our chances of winning were getting better and better. Each number created havoc in the family owning the ticket. We could see the families through the tax-office window, walking outside toward home full of disappointment. Cars were driving off. The raffle continued. There were about twenty families left. Father Zavala reached in and looked at the ticket. He read off the numbers slowly, with more emphasis now for dramatic effect. The first four numbers were ours as we looked at the ticket in my grandfather's hand. Then he hesitated and read the last number. He missed us by one! We yelled in relief. We all sighed and sat back down. More numbers. These were easier. None of them started with our number and we could relax. More people left. We were down to five families. The large tax office looked abandoned. Father Zavala reached inside and pulled a stub. The first three numbers were identical to ours and we squeezed hands and prayed with all our might, with our eyes closed, that God would not disappoint us. The next number was different from ours and we gave out a scream. My grandfather, who suffered from a bad heart, was breathing heavily. His palms were perspiring. He moved the ticket from hand to hand. The next numbers were far off from ours. Now there were only two families—ourselves and a couple with one boy and three girls. Their faces were ashen as I'm sure were ours. Father Zavala said that there should be no bad feelings for the winner. He stuck his hand into the box and came out with a stub. He started reading the numbers slowly. So far every number matched ours. On he went. The third number. The fourth. And then the fifth. It was ours. We had lost.

On the way home, my grandfather, an expert at failure, tried to console us. "That is the way life is," he said. "You never win. Life is one failure after another. Look at me. Don't you think I would like to have a good job? Oh, sometimes you can come close, but usually one never wins. You have got to get used to misfortune in life. Once in a great while you find yourself in some luck. But don't depend on it."

He kept trying to comfort us, but it was no use. Our hearts were broken. We had seen the pony being ridden away by the little boy, his father holding on to the bridle, his sisters walking behind crying because they couldn't be the first to ride him. Maggie began to cry, and when my grandfather went to her to embrace her, Cota began to cry. Then Frances. Then Sylvia. And on down the line. In a few steps we were all crying.

"A horse is a terrible thing to have," my grandfather explained, trying to ease our pain as we headed for home. He was holding Maggie's and Cota's hands. "Just think. You have to feed it at least twice a day. Water it all day long. You have to brush him to make him look pretty. You have to clean out the stable every day. A horse costs a lot of money to keep. They get worms. They get sick. They die. Heaven forbid that you children have to dig a grave for a horse. Now a goat...that's a different thing. A goat gives milk. It has babies. The babies grow up and give milk. You can eat a goat. You can't eat a horse. And besides...did you notice how poorly behaved the pony was? A horse that kicks and bites is not a friend. It's a weapon. He could have hurt one of you. I'm glad we didn't win after seeing the pony's disposition."

At that moment, no amount of logic could have convinced us that the pony was not the most precious thing to own. How we had prayed to own it. How we had planned. We had everything in place. The wood for the pen. We had started the post holes. The bucket for the feed. A little trough for the water. A water hose from the outside faucet to the pen to water and bathe the pony. What arguments we had had about him. Up to this morning, I had not lost the hope we could name him Blaze. We could turn around and still see off in the distance the little boy on the horse, his father leading him by the bridle. The scene only prolonged the agony of the morning.

My grandmother and mother were waiting in the kitchen. They had seen us walk into the yard, crying, without the horse. To them it was a relief and not a disappointment. My father was particularly overjoyed when he came in from work to find we had not won. He knew it would have been up to him to take care of the pony after the newness wore off.

On Sunday my grandfather and father fixed the lights on the car and my grandfather took off for San Antonio. By then he seemed to have forgotten about the pony. He and my father had learned through the years not to dwell on disappointments. We, in turn, felt as though someone in the family had died.

On Friday night my grandfather drove in and he was smiling. He had a surprise for us. He made us close our eyes and walk to the car. We could smell the surprise before we saw it. He had bought us a Billy goat and a nanny goat in San Antonio and had brought them all the way over in the back seat of the car.

"Now," he said, giving us the rope to lead the goats away, "if you children want to play farmers, do it with something productive and not with the most useless animal on the farm. Put the rascal in with the goat and watch the babies come."

But this was not like caring for a horse. We argued about not wanting to feed and clean it.

The pony was sold and raffled many times. Not only was it a nuisance, it was dangerous.

We quickly forgot about the pony and went on to other things. My grandmother had to take up the chore of raising the goats. "Just think what would have happened with the pony," she would remind my grandfather, rolling her eyes in front of us.

And he would always reply, "You wouldn't be alive today."

We Almost Kill Our Mother

We had come back from a track meet at the high school and decided we would have our own track meet between my parent's and my grandmother's house. But then, like it always happened, things got out of hand. We got carried away with ourselves, our delusions exceeded our boundaries. Before the first event, we needed more space. We needed the whole city block to run around.

Juan and Matías were the judges for the running events, and they made us run around the block four times. That was a mile, they said. As I think about it now, it was more like two miles. We started at the corner where my grandmother's house stood, ran past our house, past Mercé's house, turned left, ran through the street where the Lubys lived, turned left again by the Lopez's house, past the Meek's house, turned left again, ran past *Tía* Virginia's house where we would steal an orange, and then back home. Our timer was Matías, standing by the kitchen window looking at my grandmother's clock on the wall and yelling out what the second hand was doing.

After the mile, we ran the sprints, a whole city block in San Diego, supposedly one hundred yards. Matías would stand at the starting line and give us the count while Juan would stand at the finish line and yell if there were any cars coming down the street so we wouldn't get run over. If he judged the race to be tight, he would stand in the middle of the street and stop the car so we could finish our race. The confused driver would look at us and wonder what we were doing streaking past the intersection in the middle of the day in the hot sun. But usually there were few cars in San Diego. If five cars went past our house in one day, we considered it too much and we'd boo the fifth driver, unless it was George B. Parr, and then we'd look down or look away because we knew if we agitated him he might get out of the car and start shooting. We knew his father, Archer, had ordered my grandmother's brother killed. Another *tío*. *Tío* Candelario Saenz.

For refreshments, when Juan and Matías decreed, we could take a break, Cota would bring out her version of Seven-Up she had mixed by copying the ingredients printed on the bottle she had found. But she didn't have carbonated water so she used water from the outside tap. She didn't have lemons or limes so she used sour oranges she stole from *Tía* Virginia's tree. She added just a pinch of sugar, all my grandmother would let her have to waste on such an ugly concoction. The recipe called for artificial coloring, and not having any, she would very carefully add a drop of mercurochrome, what we thought in those days was *sangre-de-chango*, monkey blood. Then, at the end, to make it fizz a little, she added a pinch of the bromo-seltzer my grandfather took at nights to help him belch my grandmother's good cooking.

We all drank Cota's mixture and licked our chops, oohing and ahhing, enjoying the way the Seven-Up tasted. And then Matías, not wanting us to rest too much, made a sound like he was blowing a whistle and it was time for the next event.

And my mother wondered why we didn't gain weight.

I shouldn't have to tell you that the big events were reserved for Juan and Matías. These were what they referred to as the manly events, where the big men participated, not the little kids like us. These events were the shot put, the high jump, discus—the field events. Thank God we had not yet seen the javelin throw. And this was our time to rest and drink what remained of Cota's Seven-Up. So we'd sit and watch Juan and Matías compete. I remember distinctly that Juan won the high jump.

On the way from the track meet, we had come by way of the creek and had cut off a long piece of bamboo that we used as a high-jump bar. Juan barely cleared three or four feet. Remember that in those days the high jumper had to land on his feet. There was no foam rubber. To land on your head would have meant a broken neck and instant death. The problem with high jumping, according to Juan and Matías, was two-fold: clearing the greatest height that you could and then preparing to land on your feet to keep from getting killed—two reasons why Juan and Matías would not allow anyone except themselves the luxury of competing. We just weren't good enough.

From the high jump, we moved over a little ways next to my grandmother's house to the shot put. We didn't have a shot put. Juan and Matías had found a chunk of concrete at the site of the old bridge and had brought it home to use as a shot put. At first, they covered it with foil from cigarette wrappers to try to make it look authentic, but the foil kept falling off, and they abandoned the idea, saying it was too much trouble just to go for looks.

Matías went first, taking his time, practicing without the concrete chunk, getting his form down. Juan was next to him, trying to imitate Matías' every move. They practiced for a while, throwing the imaginary shot over and over again. Finally, when Matías thought he was good and warmed up, he reached down and picked up the chunk of concrete and stepped into the ring we had drawn on the ground with a nail. He reared back and threw the concrete a good distance, and we all laid aside our Seven-Up and applauded. Next, Juan stepped into the ring and began practicing his imaginary throws while Matías went and brought back the shot. He handed over the shot to Juan and challenged, "Beat that." He faced us and took a long bow, his pants creeping up to show he wore no socks.

Not to be outdone, Juan took the concrete, nestled it against his ear, and crouched down on one leg at the back of the ring. He gave several grunts like he had heard at the track meet and then began to hop his way across the ring on the one leg. Finally, before he stepped out, his arm flashed out like a piston, pushing the chunk of concrete with all his might. We all sat and drank our Seven Up and watched the concrete sail from Juan's hand upward into the air, seemingly as light as a feather.

My mother had been at my grandmother's next door, probably looking for something which belonged to her that my grandmother had borrowed. She had no idea what we were doing. Had she known, she would have been more careful in coming out through the kitchen door.

As she came out, she saw us all sitting down, for once, and she smiled. Had she looked up she would have seen the chunk of concrete sailing toward her. She took another step down as though she had intentionally wanted to be placed directly in the line of fire. She took the other step and then looked at us again and smiled, wondering what it was that we were doing, all sitting down, our faces twisted in horror, Juan frozen, about to cover his eyes. We could tell that she dismissed a certain thought at the time, a thought she had entertained only for an instant, a thought of God knows what. We never found out.

I am not a physicist, but I know there is a law of trajectories. Nor can I describe to you, as would a ballistic expert, the exact flight of this missile. But I can tell you that the trajectory of the chunk of concrete was such that had our mother moved a few inches either way she would not have been hit on top of the head. But she didn't. She just stood there and grinned as the object dropped on her head from the sky.

The next we knew she was on the ground lifeless, bleeding from the top of her head. My grandmother had seen everything from the kitchen door. When she saw the concrete flying through the air, she was paralyzed in fear, hoping, of course, that the projectile would miss her eldest daughter. But it was not to be. It hit her squarely on the top of the head, and when it did, my grandmother let out a scream. And when my mother fell like a dropped bird, my grandmother let out another scream that brought out Father Zavala from the rectory a block away.

We, of course, did what we always did. We ran.

Father Zavala held the back door open and smelled the air like a deer, as he had the habit of doing, trying to sense the direction from which the trouble came. He followed his nose toward my grandmother's house.

We ran past Father Zavala by the church on our way to the creek. Father Zavala turned around to ask something, but we lowered our heads, ignored him, and left him standing there, turning in circles in the confusion of the moment. Running down the street, it was Juan first, followed by Matías, then came Cota, next Frances, then Maggie, then my brother Richard, and then me. My sister Sylvia, wise beyond her years, had run in the opposite direction, toward our house, and was now safely in her room looking out through the window. As I brought up the rear, I could hear all the huffing and puffing, the excessive rubbing of denim coveralls, from up front. I was used to running errands and was in excellent

shape. By the time we got to the cave at the creek, I was leading the pack.

When Father Zavala arrived, he was greeted with the
spectacle of my grandmother in her favorite role—beating her
chest in agony like she enjoyed doing—acting like the Virgin
Mary holding the crucified Christ, my mother, in her arms.

Father Zavala found my mother's head covered in blood.
He had the presence of mind to check her pulse. "She is all
right," he reassured my grandmother. My mother opened one
eye and asked, "Dr. Dunlap?"

We could see from the top of the creek bank all the way to
the house. As we sat in silence, worried about what would
happen to us, we saw Father Zavala and my grandmother
stand my mother on her feet and walk her inside the house.
Tía Virginia, who had the only phone in the neighborhood,
must have heard the screams and called the doctor because
Dr. Dunlap arrived in his large green Buick, stayed for about
ten minutes and then came out, got in his car, and drove off.
Tía Virginia then came out of the house and hurried across
the yard to see what had happened, followed by *Tía* Alicia,
Tía Chata, and *Tía* Mina, all emerging out of their homes like
disturbed bees and then disappearing into my grandmother's
house.

Father Zavala came out wringing his hands. He descended the steps, walked over to the chunk of concrete and picked
it up. He examined it from several angles and then threw it
away, farther than Juan or Matías had done.

We had to return some day, so we decided to get back
home that night. We arrived quietly in the dark, trying to
sneak in, but my grandmother was waiting with her broom.

No one can stay angry forever, not over the same thing
anyway. On the other hand, forgiveness never comes like
thunder, either. It was a gradual experience for us, meant to
punish us over a period of time. First, while we encouraged
him, Juan had to crawl through the cobwebs, spiders, ants,
and some snakes under the house every day to get the few
eggs from the chickens that roosted there. Then we had to
run to the bakery three times a day—before every meal—to
buy bread. Then Cota and Maggie and Frances had to sweep
the yard every morning and again at night. All of us, except
Sylvia, had to clean up the little shed where my grandmother
and my mother stored things, where our uncles stored their

slight possessions whenever they moved. It took us days to get everything out, then clean the shed, and then put everything back. Gradually, we did less and less until we did nothing except discuss our next plan. And eventually things were back to normal. My grandmother never forgave us completely, though. From then on, all our track meets were held on the parish church grounds. "Go bother the priest," she would tell us. "He doesn't have anything to do anyway. Maybe some of his good can rub off on you."

My mother never remembered what happened, and we did not volunteer the information. What a relief it was when Dr. Dunlap said she would not suffer any permanent damage. She did walk around a little disoriented for a few days, but then she was herself again.

We were at the cave by the creek smoking one day when Juan and Matías reminded us that it was a good thing the concrete hadn't hit my mother on the *cien*, the "hundred," the small area between the eye and the ear all of us believed was the weakest part of the head. All you had to do was punch someone on the *cien* and that was it. It meant instant death. It was the same as stabbing someone in the navel with a straight pin, letting out all the body air a person is born with, making him flitter away and die like a collapsed balloon. But that's another story.

"None of us would be alive today," Cota reminded us, very seriously, passing the cigarette around.

We gave up track as being too dangerous for the spectators and too strenuous for us. We preferred baseball. Baseball was more of a game of skill and intelligence, as our Uncle Adolfo was fond of telling us.

"Even a dog has better sense than to run around the block like you children do," he said.

El Negro Joe

El Negro Joe was from Alice. He had been working in Alice for the same restaurant for many years, but when his health broke down and he started missing a lot of days, he was let go. He heard there was work at the San Diego Cafe, so he drove down one day, showed them how he cooked, and he was hired.

At first he'd drive the ten miles back and forth every day, but then the strain started to get to him. He'd have to get up at four in the morning to get to work at five. At night, after everyone had gone, he'd have to clean the kitchen, get in his old car and drive back, and he wouldn't get home until one.

One day he asked for the afternoon off, just between lunch and dinner time, to give him a chance to look for a place to stay in San Diego.

We were playing outside when we saw him slowly drive by, looking into our yard. We had no idea what he was up to. He drove to the corner and then stopped and backed up. He came up the driveway and got off, a big man with a large pot belly, smoking a cigar, wearing brown pants, black shoes, white socks, a faded white shirt, and a short tie that only reached the middle of his belly. Large, broad yellow suspenders held up his pants. He wore a wide, cream panama hat tilted over to one side. The shadow from the hat cast a blackness over his face. Added to his own blackness, it made the features of his face disappear, except for the gold tooth shining when he smiled. When he finally took off his hat, we were fascinated by a long deep scar on the right side of his face. It extended down his cheek from above the ear to his chin, a souvenir of a fight long ago in a bar in San Antonio. "Over a wemmin," he would tell us later when we got to know him better. He never explained more than that, but he seemed to know a lot of black women in Alice and Corpus Christi.

This was the first black man we had ever seen up close. We followed him toward the house and stood behind while he knocked at my grandmother's kitchen door. He knocked again and got no answer. He turned around and had to notice our curiosity. He couldn't resist. He gave us his favorite ugly stare and yelled, "Boo!" at us and we ran off a short distance. Then he started to laugh, exposing his gold tooth. We started to laugh with him.

Juan ran up to the door, opened it, and went inside to look for his mother. The rest of us were staring at the man. He looked around and took his cigar out of his mouth.

"What you chillun lookin' at?" he asked. "Ain't you ever seen a negro before?"

Juan came out with my grandmother. She asked him in Spanish what he wanted, and he answered in crude Spanish that he was looking for a place to stay. My grandmother told him he could not stay with her.

He understood, he said, that he could not live with white people, but he had seen the shed at the back of the yard and wondered if he could stay there.

My grandmother thought about it for a while and said we were using the shed for storage. And even if we were not, she would have to ask my grandfather who was working in San Antonio before she could make a decision.

El Negro Joe spoke in English. He understood she could not allow a black man to live close by without her husband's approval, and he wanted to know if possibly she could get an answer from her husband soon. He was a good and decent man. If my grandmother wanted, he could help her clean the shed out. He could do anything, he said. He was a carpenter, a plumber, an electrician, and he was desperate for a place.

My grandmother asked us what he had said and we told her, each of us excitedly trying to get a word into the conversation.

El Negro Joe turned around once more and smiled at us. This time, we returned the smile. He seemed a good enough man. When he reached up to take off his panama to wipe his brow with his sleeve, we noticed the scars on his hands. "A fight wif a man on account of a wemmin," he was to tell us.

He wanted to know if he could stay there the same night while my grandmother got word from our grandfather.

My grandmother shook her head when we explained what he wanted. "Tell him," she said in Spanish, "that I cannot. My husband would have to be the one to approve such a thing."

El Negro Joe smiled pleasantly when we told him what our grandmother had said. "I kinda got the drif'," he said.

We followed him back to the car. Before taking off, he tipped his hat at us. We started to laugh, and he gave us a mean stare once more and then, without warning, he yelled "Boo!" at us again. This time we did not run. He was laughing so hard he had to hold his stomach. Then he started to cough. He spat blood on the dirt, got in the car and smiling waved at us with his cigar. By then we were laughing with him.

Two days later El Negro Joe returned. My grandmother had not heard from my grandfather and didn't know when she would.

"The letter then woulda took a week," he said. He looked about, pursing his lips, the cigar between his fingers. He coughed slightly, taking out his handkerchief as he did so. He spat into it. "Maybe I could jest sit on the porch awhile jus' to res'," he kept on. He backed up to the stairs and sat down very slowly. "Jez give me a minute an' I'll be fine," he said.

Every day he would come to ask about the letter and with each day we came to like the old man more and more. He just didn't come and go. He would have to rest, and while doing so, he would tell us things, stories we found interesting and funny. The whole family felt sorry for him not having a place to stay and having such poor health.

A week later my grandmother received the letter. My grandfather knew El Negro Joe from Alice when my grandfather had managed the Travelers Hotel at the bus station. El Negro Joe, he wrote, had been the cook at the City Cafe next door. He didn't see why the man couldn't stay in the shed.

We were so excited when we heard the news. El Negro Joe was coming to live with us. We would be the only family in town with a black man. We took off running to the San Diego Cafe to give him the good news. We found him behind the hot stove, four gas burners going at once, a towel around his neck, his panama resting on his head, the hissing sounds of fat burning on a large griddle—hamburgers, bacon, eggs, pancakes—the gurgling of the deep fat fryer and the smell of french fries and chicken fried steak. He was cooking them all at the same time. He had one big window fan sucking out hot air, but the kitchen heat was almost unbearable. Regardless of the heat, I thought that this man had the most wonderful job in the world to be able to be around so much good food.

We gave him the word. He could come live with us. He gave out a happy little whooping sound. He was in better health today.

Our grandfather knew him from the City Cafe. Who was our grandfather? Gonzalo. He remembered my grandfather. A good man. "Not good wif the dollar, or wif the wimmen," he said. He had my grandfather judged right.

Juan and Matías got close to him and he took out some french fries with a long fork and flipped them over to them. They caught the hot fried potatoes, but had to juggle them to keep from blistering their hands.

The rest of the day my grandmother, my mother, Juan, Matías, Cota, Maggie, Frances, Sylvia, Richard and I worked hard to get the little shed ready for El Negro Joe. We took everything out. With my grandmother's supervision, we culled what needed to go back inside and took the rest and put it in my grandmother's house. My grandmother had an iron cot she kept at my Uncle Mercé's and we brought it over, rinsed it off with the hose, dried it out in the sun, and placed it inside the shed. We dusted off an old mattress which Mercé didn't use anymore, brought it back with us, and beat it clean on the clothes line until we were exhausted. Then my grandmother sprayed it with kerosene to kill the bedbugs. We moved an old metal trunk from Mercé's and placed it by the side of the bed. On top of the trunk we set a kerosene lantern. The shed had a concrete shower and we cleaned it out and ran water through it for a while, until the water came out through the drainage pipe behind the shed.

We were waiting up for El Negro Joe when he drove in after midnight. He was surprised to see us. He took his cigar out of his mouth and gave out his strong laugh, shaking his belly and coughing at the end. We showed him in, showed him his bed, the mattress, the metal trunk, and the kerosene lamp we had lit for him. He sat on the bed and pulled off his shoes and wiggled his toes through his socks. He took off his socks and rubbed his toes. We had never seen feet so black in our lives. He caught on that we were staring at him and he smiled. "Well, chillun," he said, gently leaning back and easing himself into bed, "I's goin' to bed. I's had a long day, and the days don' get shorta with age."

I don't know why, but we had expected to see quite a bit of El Negro Joe. But we didn't. He would get up very early, at around four-thirty and come in very late. And even the times when we did stay up waiting for him, he would be so tired he would excuse himself and fall asleep rubbing his toes while we stood by the iron cot watching him.

One morning when we were playing at the courthouse, we saw him driving toward the house. We stopped him and he gave us a ride back home. We were jumping up and down inside the car that smelled heavily like funeral wreaths. We had not noticed that El Negro Joe was in pain. He was not feeling well. By the time we got home, he was spitting up blood.

My grandmother didn't want to nurse him. She had enough to do without taking on another man whom she hardly knew. But as the days went by and she saw us coming in and out of the shed, she began to take more of an interest.

"How is he doing?" she asked us.

Matías replied, "He doesn't look good, Mama. He's hungry and he might die."

"Right here on my property?" she asked, as though that were enough reason for him not to die.

"Yes," Cota said. "He might die."

Juan said, "He's spitting up blood, Mama. He looks bad."

"If he dies here," my grandmother thought half-aloud, "then what are we to do with him?"

"Bury him," Matías said, and we started to laugh.

"Don't you laugh," my grandmother scolded us. "God might punish you and make you sicker than him."

That was always good for a scare.

My grandmother went back inside the house, leaving us standing on the porch thinking of what we could do with El Negro Joe. He needed food. My mother was working, and she couldn't be bothered. My father was working in Alice, and he came in late from work and left early, just like El Negro Joe. He hardly knew the old man.

My grandmother stuck her head out through the door and asked, "Is he really that sick?"

"Yes," we all answered.

"Well," my grandmother said, "just this once I'll go take a look at him."

She went back inside and came out with her bonnet. She said, "I don't know how you children get me involved in things. I wish to God I could leave you children alone to suffer on your own." She stopped suddenly. "What will the neighbors say? Me going into that shack to see a black man."

"Who cares, Mama," Maggie said, waving her little hand at her mother to keep her going on her way. "He's real sick."

"Well," my grandmother said after a while, "now that I'm halfway there I have to go. And I don't want any of you saying anything to him about me taking care of him and nursing him and all that. I don't want to clean him up. Remember that he's black."

"He's not black," Matías replied. "He's more like brown."

My grandmother said, "Be quiet, Matías. Don't be smart with me."

Every morning my grandmother cooked something for him and made sure he was clean. We helped him up, and he was able to go to the outdoor toilet. He would bathe in the concrete shower in the shed. She cooked for him at noon, and in the afternoon we would sit him under the shade of the salt cedars. He was not smoking by then. Later, he would eat again, and we would put him to bed. He missed so much work that he had been fired, and the battery in his car had gone dead.

One morning the restaurant owner came by to see my grandmother to tell her that he thought El Negro Joe might have tuberculosis. "I had a brother die of tuberculosis. You wouldn't want to be around anyone with tuberculosis, María," he said. "Especially the children."

That left my grandmother wondering what to do with El Negro Joe.

"In a week he has to leave," she said to us. "Go tell him."

El Negro Joe couldn't get up from his iron bed. He tried to prop himself up on his elbow, but even that failed. "I'll go," he said. "I understan' what María wants. I'm not in good health. Good Lord, if'n you take me, make it soon so's I's don' have to suffer no mo'."

El Negro Joe was an incredibly strong man. In one week, he was able to walk outside on his own to sit under the salt cedars to watch us play. He was able to take the battery out of his car, and we hauled it in the wagon to the gas station and had it recharged. He was back to smoking his ugly black cigars.

At night, El Negro Joe would sit around and listen to our grandmother and whoever else happened to be staying at my grandmother's house tell stories about the old days. He understood enough Spanish to laugh at the right places.

This night it had been a story of how scared my grandmother had been one night at the ranch when the wolves seemed to be howling her name. El Negro Joe was sitting with us children. He was shaking his head as though completely frightened. When my grandmother was through, she asked if El Negro Joe had a story he wanted to tell, a story of being scared.

Before he could start, my Uncle Mercé had one of his fits and began to curse. In the middle of the fit, Mercé decided to run off toward town. Out of deference to El Negro Joe, we ignored Mercé and directed our attention to the black man.

"As a chile?" he asked slowly. "Scared? Lawdy, lawdy. Scared you say? Let me see...There's so many stories of being scared when you is a Negro. There's one when I was in Alice one night and some men followed me to kill me. But that wasn't when I was a chile. Happened just a few years ago. Didn't want no Negro working at the cafe. But that ain't nuthin'. That happens all the time. Never can go no place decent. You understan'?" He took off his panama and laid it on his lap. He had a faraway look in his eyes which we could see by the moonlight. We could tell he was arranging his thoughts.

"He's going to tell us a good story," my grandmother said.

"Well," El Negro Joe said, "I can't tell this one in Mexican. I don' have all the words I need."

"Tell it in English," my mother said. "Someone will help María out".

"Qué dice?" my grandmother asked. We told her El Negro Joe was going to tell us a story, but it had to be in English.

Cota went and sat by her to translate El Negro Joe's story.

El Negro Joe leaned forward in his chair. He scrubbed the fire out of his cigar against the sole of his shoe.

"Scared?" he asked once more. He spat on the ground and slowly moved his head sideways like he was resting it on his shoulder. "Let me tell you. When I were a li'l chile like 'im over there," he began, pointing his finger at me, "my pa' couldn't find no work, no ways, nowhere. We were livin' on a farm outside of Karnes City. We had no crops that year. Couldn't afford to go half on seed. One morning some men come for my pa' and he leaves with 'em. They is goin' to look for work they say. But my mama, she knows they ain't goin' to look for work. They is tired of lookin' and they is goin' 'round town lookin' for trouble. That night he don't show up, and we figure he's out in some joint havin' a good time 'cause that was the way he was. Havin' a good time with good-time wemmin. Anyways, my mama and my grandmama and all us kids—we was eight—we couldn't git to sleep that night 'cause the grown wemmin was pacin' up and down the room and we could see from under the sheets the shadows they made back and forth, and they was talkin' in whispers an' then we could hear my mother crying softly, like a little bird, mind you. Not no squeal cryin' like the Mexicans do when somebody dies. Oh yes, we cry and carry on, but, lawdy, when the Mexican wemmin gets to crying at a funeral—well, there ain't nothin' like it. We was scared 'cause we knew somethin' was awfully wrong. In the middle of the night we hear a shot—something go bang! Real loud. Like a gun going off, and my mama was sitting down next to my grandmama by the door, and they shot up from the chairs like they heard a ghost call they's name. They go 'round the house runnin' and yellin' almos' like the Mexican wemmin. We chillun get up an' my blest mama, she tells us to get back under the sheets and not to look outa the window. We hear the men talkin' oukside and the dogs growlin' like theys someone in the yard they don' like. My mama an' my grandmama don' know what to do— iffen theys beposed to run or stay or what? Then my grand-mama cain't control herself no way an' she screams about sumpin' an' my mama, she runs to the window to see an' she screams a scream I never can get outa my mind. We look ouk-side to see what the commotion is all about. My pa' is being beat up by some white folks. They is kickin' 'im an hittin' 'im with sticks. We start to scream when we see our pa' rolling in the dirt by the light of the cars. Then we see this white man acomin' with a rope an' they tie my pa' up an' we is screamin' for 'em to leave my pa' alone but we don't come out cause they is too many and we get it too. You know what I mean? We'd be kilt. My mama is goin' crazy lookin' out the window. My grandmama, bless her soul, too. She is long gone to Heaven like my Mama. She is goin' crazy beatin' her chest. Then my mama cain't stand it no mo'. She throws the door open, pushes my grandmama out of the way, and runs oukside to help my pa'. My grandmama runs after her, shoutin' for her to come back. 'They is gonna kill you too!' she's shoutin' over and over again. One of the white folks jumps my mama an' knocks her down and then starts to kick 'er. They throw 'er 'round like rag doll. We is screamin' inside lookin' outa the window. 'Let my mama alone!' we yell. 'Let my pa' alone!,' we yell. They's got my mama down and are tearin' her clothes offen her. My grandmama is fightin' them, but they hit her on the head wif a board. They's put a rope around my pa's neck and throw the rope over the branch of the tree. Four or five of 'em start pulling on the rope, and we watch my mama on the ground draggin' hersef to my pa', screamin'. They take my mama and hold her down and one man starts doin' something to her. We was too little to know. My grandmama is beatin' her chest. My pa's hangin' from the rope slowly goin' up the tree, shaking his whole body like his body cain't stand what's happen' to 'it."

El Negro Joe stopped to wipe the tears from his eyes. We didn't know who to look at, El Negro Joe who seemed consumed in the story or my grandmother who was getting the story second hand from Cota. We could tell she was carried away with the events.

"Did they kill him?" my mother asked, finally.

El Negro Joe relit his cigar and crossed his leg. "Yes," he answered, studying the ember on the tip of his cigar, "they kilt 'im. The men left after they did what they wanted to my mama. We spent the whole night lookin' out the window at him hangin' from the tree afeerd to go out and cut 'im down. We cut my pa down in the mornin'. We didn't wait for sun up, either. We packed everythin' we owned and took off. Eight chillun. My mama and my grandmama. Traveled all day till we got to Alice where my mama had a sister. My mama then had a boy, my brother Monro, from the white men. He was half-white. He worked at the barbershop, sweepin' floors and shinin' shoes. Everybody died in Alice. My grandmama died right away from her heart. My mama was next. When Monro was about ten. All the chillun are gone except me. I'm the one lived the longest. And I ain't got much to go."

My grandmother looked very seriously at El Negro Joe. She was awed by his misfortunes. She said, "This man has suffered more than Jesus Christ."

It was getting late and we could see Mercé returning from town, having finished with his fit.

El Negro Joe got his car running and left shortly after that night; went back to Alice for a short while and from there we heard he had gone to Karnes City where his family was from originally. He was living on a farm by himself. We never heard from him again.

We did remember him occasionally when someone told a story of outrageous suffering. "That's a Negro-Joe story," we would say.

During the lull in the conversation which inevitably followed as we thought of him, my grandmother would say, "I wonder where he is? Telling someone his story about his family. How cruel some people are just because of the color of a man's skin. Sometimes I wonder if there is a God."

Boxing

We never had a newspaper in San Diego. We didn't have to. All the daily news was passed on by word of mouth. And, of course, there were several people in the town who were more respected as chroniclers of the news than others. For example, a distant uncle just couldn't help being a liar and he delighted in making up stories—lies about someone dying, someone running off with another woman, someone in jail—passing them on around the streets in the early morning and then waiting during the day for the lie to take hold. These lies were called *borregos*, or sheep, for reasons known only to the old people of the town. My mother hated this uncle for having this flaw in his character. "I can't stand him...not even in a photograph," she would say.

Alfredo Gomez, on the other hand, was reliable...and good. You could believe everything he told my father. But of all of them, the chroniclers of the town, the most respected and revered was *Tío* Amando, the butcher. My father would get up very early to go to work in Alice, but before he left, even before breakfast, he would drive to *Tío* Amando's and listen to the morning news as *Tío* Amando and his son Amandito butchered the beef for the day. *Tío* Amando, through his network, which included Alfredo Gomez, knew exactly what had happened during the night while we had been happily asleep. He knew the inside of politics, who was composing lampoons for whom, who was having affairs, who had been in a fight in what beer joint, and lastly, the worst of all, who had gotten killed in a fight. Then to complete the format of his oral newspaper with a comic section, he would throw in the latest one or two jokes. My father would come home from the meat market, sit down and eat breakfast, and tell us all that *Tío* Amando had reported for the day.

In those days I had made up my mind that I wanted to be a boxer. Every Friday night Matías, Juan, Richard and I would sit by the radio, the room darkened for effect, and listen to the fights. The names were so good: Joe Louis, Sugar Ray Robinson, Jake LaMotta, Billy Conn. I wanted to be Kid Gavilan. I wanted to be a fighter. There was nothing in the world that I wanted more. I would shadowbox during the matches. Every jab thrown over the radio I would throw in turn. The uppercuts. The overhand rights. Sugar Ray's deadly left hook. I went around the house throwing punches in the air.

My grandmother thought that I was crazy. "The child has gone crazy," she said. "But just you hit something in this house and break it and let's see what a fighter you are," she warned me. My mother, hearing the warning, agreed. "That goes for me, too," she said.

That summer we worked the milk-bottle concession stand at the annual Cotton Fiesta. And with the money, I ordered two pairs of boxing gloves from the back of a Captain Marvel comic book. I waited for months for the gloves, and when they arrived, my mother had a fit. She did not agree with what I had done. I had bought, with hard earned money, two pair of boxing gloves made of cardboard leather. My grandmother was more understanding and I was allowed to keep the gloves. My brother Richard and I would box in the yard. Matías and Juan worked the corners. Cota was the referee and the rest of the children were the audience. Slowly, painfully, we watched the gloves unraveling as we fought. My brother Richard was left handed, and we could never figure out what he was doing.

That was the least of my problems though. I had the habit of closing my eyes when I boxed. Besides, I lowered my head as though I was going to butt my opponent, and in this position, with my eyes closed, flailing away at the air, I was an easy target for anyone. Everyone agreed I needed more work or I was going to get hurt seriously.

My life changed though one Saturday afternoon in the old movie house. The Pathe Newsreel came on, and there on the screen was Sugar Ray Robinson training. I was mesmerized by the talent of the man. I wanted to be Sugar Ray Robinson.

He was hitting a punching bag with blinding hand speed and with a smoothness of rhythm that I found unbelievable. He was doing all of this and looking at the camera and grinning! We had found the solution to my problem. I needed to train on a punching bag.

Which is where *Tío* Amando comes in.

Tío Amando worked his butcher shop on demand. Since his refrigerator was very small, nothing was killed and butchered unless he was running out. In other words, if he didn't have what you wanted, you bought what he had. Nobody had ever heard of sirloin or rib-eye. I don't know what ever happened to those cuts of meat. They must have been there. Every cow is the same. But we never saw those cuts of meat. They disappeared mysteriously when he butchered. He did delight in selling my father the spleen, an organ so tough and indigestible that it required hours of boiling and a very long time to chew and assimilate. "So that you can make saliva," he would say, slapping the package as he handed it to my father.

When he needed to butcher an animal, he and his son would get up early, drive to his ranch just outside of town, and slaughter what they felt they could sell. They would haul the carcass into town on the back of the pick-up truck and cut it right there behind the cooler. And all the time, *Tío* Amando was gathering his news from the locals who came by, stopping now and then to give a couple of whacks to his knife against the cold steel. By seven in the morning, he was so full of news he could burst.

One Saturday afternoon my father showed up with a big grin on his face. He had a surprise for me wrapped in butcher paper. He explained to my mother that he had told *Tío* Amando of my predicament—that I wanted a punching bag— and *Tío* Amando had thought for awhile, rubbed the stubble on his chin, and said, "I'll take care of the little scoundrel." He reached into the cooler and grabbed the hind end of the cow, cut into it, and placed the fat-covered piece on the butcher block. Very carefully, my father watched as Tío Amando dissected the fat of the organ. When he was through, he wrapped it for my father to take home.

Now my father grinned happily as he placed the package on the kitchen table, my brother Richard and my sister Sylvia and I waiting patiently for him to open it up. My heart jumped in the joy of anticipation as he unfolded the paper and unwrapped the contents. Before us on the table we saw for the first time an indefinable mass of gray tissue. My father picked it up.

"What in the world is it?" my grandmother asked.

"The bladder of the cow," my father answered.

"How ugly," my mother said. "What is it for?"

"For the next boxing champion of the world," my dad said.

My brother and my sister made some excuse and left my father and I studying the problem. I knew they had run to tell the others about my punching bag. My mother went outside to water some plants. She knew my father's and *Tío* Amando's problem-solving mentality.

My father was very excited, much more so than I. But what could I do? I didn't want to hurt his feelings. I had considered in my mind something better to strike at than the urinary bladder of a cow. I stuck around and we stripped some more fat off the bladder so that at least it looked as if it had possibilities. It was round, sturdy, leathery. When we were through, my father looked at me and then at the mass of tissue before us. I knew what he was thinking. Who was going to inflate it? There should have been no question. It being Saturday, he already had a few dozen beers in him. So without hesitating, he took the bladder, held it to his mouth, and began to blow into it. After each breath, he spat out the door. Outside we could hear the voices from the other children. They were waiting patiently for me to come out with my prize.

The smell was unbelievable. It went beyond ammonia. My father blew it up as fast and as hard as he could so he would not have to do it again. He ran around the kitchen looking for a string. We finally found a piece of twine in one of the drawers. Quickly, he tied off the end, making several loops around to make sure the air would not escape. He handed the bladder to me and walked slowly to the kitchen door. I knew what was awaiting me.

I stepped out, holding the bladder over my head, acting as though I loved it. The others didn't know what to make of it. They had expected me to be ashamed, but I was not about to give them that pleasure.

I ran around the yard with it as though it was the most beautiful balloon. Immediately the smell of urine overtook the yard.

My dad came out with another piece of twine and tied it around the narrow end again, just to be sure. I had, what looked to him, the perfect punching bag. We walked over the yard wondering where we could hang it, and eventually we agreed on the clothesline. While everyone watched, he tied it there, and we both stepped back to admire the way it looked almost translucent, like a balloon made of animal parts rocking gently in the breeze. He said, while admiring his work, "Tío Amando was right. It's perfect. Wait until I tell him tomorrow morning."

I went over to the bladder, reached back, and hit it with all my might, my eyes wide open. Secretly, I was hoping the whole thing would explode and then we could throw it away. The impact of the blow sent the bladder spinning around the clothesline and the old remnants of urine flying in all directions, burning my eyes. I spat, smelled my hand and made a face. "Don't worry," my father advised me, "that will go away after a while...It has to. Nothing lasts forever."

I stayed there and hit it several more times, respectfully this time, more light taps than the heavy blow I had first given it. I was no fool. I asked if anyone else wanted to hit it and everyone backed off.

The next day I had a full audience. I could hit it harder, but the air somehow was escaping and with my father gone, I was left to inflate it myself. When I did, I tasted the bitterness of urine that had impregnated the old bladder since the moment the animal was slaughtered. I realized then how much my father loved me to have been the first one to blow it up. I knew then that I could never let him down.

From that day on, encouraged by Juan, Matías, Cota, Maggie, Frances, Sylvia, and Richard, I would dance around the bladder, now light and flapping in the wind, tapping it lightly just like Sugar Ray Robinson had done, and in time, the smell was gone, the smell from my hands was gone, and every time I hit it, I rejoiced in the whomping sound it made.

Now that it was cured, everyone wanted to punch it.

In time, the bladder became dry and translucent. We could see through it, and every day that we hit it, it would resound even more, like a tympani, filling the neighborhood with a melodic bass. Neighbors would come out to see what could possibly be making this jungle-like sound.

We took the old gloves and went around the neighborhood looking for fights for me. The only time anyone accepted the challenge was a disaster. I had never seen anyone with the hand speed of this kid. Every time I tried to hit him, he hit me five times. Once the word got out, everyone wanted to fight me. My nose bled all the time, and my mother forbade me to ever box again. Juan and Matías wanted to retire me at an early age, and my mother burned the gloves. The cow bladder stayed on the clothesline where we would play with it, making it emit strange sounds by hitting it with different force.

I was not through being embarrassed. Every time he saw me, *Tío* Amando would take up a boxer's stance and jab at me and say, "Come on. Throw your best at the old man. Let's see how well you can do. Let's see if all that training your father brags about is making you better."

"He's getting better," my father would say. We both knew he was lying. He, along with everyone else, knew I had gotten worse. The fear of getting hit was overpowering. I continued to fight by myself, a sort of charade, flailing away at the air without fear of retaliation. I boxed less and less, played more marbles. The old urine soaked bladder was getting more of a beating from the wind than from me. The others, mercifully, let me bury my dream without too much abuse. Still they would not let me take the bladder down, just to remind me of how dumb I could be.

My father was oblivious to the fact that I had given up my dream. Several times he wanted to know if I wanted another bladder. *Tío* Amando had saved one for me.

"If he's champion one day, Gonzalo," *Tío* Amando said, "look at the stories we can tell. Trained with the bladder of a cow."

I could hear the snickering behind me from Juan and Matías, Cota, Maggie, Frances, Sylvia and Richard. I was never to completely live this foolish dream down.

It did endear me to the adults. I never asked for anything else again.

The Sacraments

In each Sacrament there is required a minister, who confers the Sacrament with the intention of doing that which the church intends...The effect of the Sacrament is ... impeded through the fault of the recipient, for example, if one feigns to receive it and with a heart unprepared to receive worthily. Such a one, although he actually receives the Sacrament, does not receive the effect of the Sacrament, that is, the grace of the Holy Spirit.

—St. Thomas Aquinas

St. Thomas wrote those words around 1270. How prophetic they would become when the time for my Confirmation arrived.

My sister Sylvia and my brother Richard had been confirmed the year before. Being older, Juan, Matías, Cota, Maggie, and Francis had all received the Sacrament. We still laughed about those times when my grandmother had to round them up on Sunday when the Bishop came from Corpus Christi to do the honors.

All of them, except me, had gone through First Communion also, although Father Zavala, when he forgot, would insist that I go to Confession with the rest of them. I never did have the heart to go to Communion though. I was afraid that in a fit of remembrance, Father Zavala would throw me out of the church.

Juan and Matías had told me stories about Confirmation. During the ceremony, I would be slapped by the Bishop so hard I would feel like my head was fifty feet wide. One little girl had been knocked out cold by the Bishop, a big burly man

who liked to squeeze children's noses much like Father
Zavala did our ears.

One of my father's favorite drinking buddies, José—
among the few that could keep up with him—was always
appointed my godfather for one thing or another. Naturally, a
few weeks before Confirmation, my father announced that
this gentleman had consented to be my godfather again, this
time for the Sacrament of Confirmation. They had decided
the night before at some tavern. The man had been more
than glad to do us the favor. As a matter of fact, his wife had
just bought him a new suit and shoes, and now he could put
them to good use.

The next Sunday when my brother and I were serving
Mass with Father Zavala, I was glad to hear him tell the
small crowd of old ladies and men that the Bishop had decided that First Holy Communions were to be administered
on the same day, killing two birds with one stone—
Confirmation and then Communion—on the same trip. He
had not wanted to come visit us twice in one year. Somehow,
the way Father Zavala explained the Bishop's words, it did
not come off as an insult to the town. My mother and grandmother were at the church, and they too heard the good news.
They were delighted. I would be drawn from my heathen
stage in one-single day.

The following weeks, my mother prepared me for both
Sacraments. At the same time, the others were trying to off-
set everything my mother was telling me. If my mother said
the Bishop would not look at me, would not ask me questions,
then Matías and Juan and Cota would tell me the Bishop
would peer into my eyes to see if I had sinned. He could tell.
That was why he was the Bishop. He was going to ask me
questions about the Catholic Church. How many apostles
really and truly loved Jesus? Why was Judas eating with the
rest of the apostles if Jesus is God and God knew everything?
If God is so smart, why didn't He tell Jesus about the plot to
kill Him? Why didn't God make Jesus disappear from wherever they didn't like him and make him reappear in San
Diego, Texas, where we all loved him? Why didn't Jesus beat
everyone up? Why is it when you kill a lamb, you kill Jesus?
Why was it a sin to cross your legs in church? Why was it a
sin, according to the nuns, to look anywhere but forward at
the altar during Mass? Why was God's name hollow and not

solid? Where was the womb, as in "fruit of the womb?" How many times had I stolen soda pop from the lady who had the grocery store in the front room of her house?

They had me worried for a while, until things got so ridiculous, and I heard them one day, laughing about my gullibility.

My mother and grandmother went to Alice and bought me a white shirt to wear. Meanwhile, to be on the safe side, I was studying the Catechism to prepare for whatever the Bishop might throw my way.

Friday night, as usual, I went with the gang to Confession just to hang around the church. I was supposed to confess my sins on Saturday, the night before the First Communion. Father Zavala appeared tired and he forgot about my First Communion. He insisted I confess my sins along with the rest of them. He had dark rings around his eyes. His normal jovial voice was raspy as though he were coming down with something. It was the Bishop's visit wearing him down, so much preparation did the Bishop require. He was very lenient with confessions this Friday night. No one received a penance of over three Hail Marys and three Our Fathers. He hardly squeezed our ears. In no time, we were playing in the park again. Even his organ playing afterwards, as we stopped to listen, seemed listless and disheartened—empty of the bravura with which he loved to embellish his music. We could not hear the thumping of his large feet on the pedals.

Saturday night before the Bishop arrived, my father and his friend celebrated my Confirmation and First Communion as though they were the ones getting the benefit of the Sacrament. We all shined our only pair of shoes, and my mother took me to Confession once more, just in case I had done something with my uncles and aunts, and brother and sister that she did not know about.

Very early Sunday morning I couldn't sleep, so I got up and dressed. I walked the yard nervously between our house and my grandmother's house, waiting for everyone else to get up, reciting my Catechism, and the Mysteries of the Rosary. I was very conscious not to swallow my saliva. To do so would break my fast. Juan, in bed, saw me through the window of his bedroom, and he whistled at how well I looked. He had never seen me dressed before. He said I looked like a girl.

Matías rolled over in bed to the window and he too began to whistle at me. I called them something and they laughed at me. They said I would have to go to confession again.

My mother had gotten up by the time I had to go back inside. I couldn't take the whistling anymore. By then, Cota, Maggie and Francis had joined in. My mother prepared breakfast and my brother and sister got up. Everyone ate in silence, although I could see my brother grinning at me for wearing a new shirt. I couldn't eat. I had to keep my fast.

An hour before the ceremony, my mother went to get my father out of bed, and my sister and brother and I went to my grandmother's house to see what the others were up to. My grandmother admired the way I looked, and the others made fun of me. My grandmother wet her index fingers with her tongue and plastered my eyebrows down with saliva. The kids laughed some more. They were ready to go to church to see me get slapped by the Bishop and possibly get embarrassed by him when he would ask me in front of the church to recite all the Mysteries of the Rosary. They didn't know I had them memorized.

Thirty minutes before the Confirmation, my godfather had not arrived. My father got in the car and went looking for him. Twenty minutes later, he returned alone. My godfather could not be found. His wife said he had gone to the taverns to cure a hangover the likes of which he had never had before. He was in no condition to appear before the Bishop. Still my father and mother had hope. My grandmother did not. She complained about the man. He had never been any good. Very untrustworthy.

My brother had gone on ahead of us to serve as an altar boy. We could hear him ringing the bell. The godparents and parents would be arriving with their children. We were still on the porch waiting to see what we would do.

My grandmother said, "Let's go. Something will happen on the way." And we left for church.

On the way, my grandmother stopped as if she had been struck with a solution. We were walking down the middle of the street, and she lined up Matías, Juan, Cota, Maggie, and Francis. My mother was complaining. We were out of time. My father had gone on, not bothering to stop. My grandmother inspected each of her children and finally said, "The one

who looks the best dressed is Matías. Let him be the godfather. The Bishop is old. He doesn't know any better."

"But he can't be a godfather," my mother complained.
"He's not old enough. He hasn't fasted. He can't take
Communion. And a godfather is supposed to take a parent's
place in case the child becomes an orphan."

Cota said, "Mary's right. Matías can't take care of himself, much less anyone else."

"And besides," said Juan, "he looks so bad. I can see all
the godfathers from here. They're wearing suits and ties."

"Well," my grandmother said, "it was just a thought."

"You wait and see," my mother said, "José will show up.
He may not be in any condition to stand up, but he'll show
up."

"God will find a way," my grandmother said. "Even if we
have to prop him up."

By the time we arrived at the front of the church, my
brother was ringing the last bell. The children, about twenty
of them, all dressed in new white shirts and new white dresses, along with their well dressed godfathers and godmothers
were lined up in front of the church. They made a beautiful
picture. The nuns were there, angry-looking, eyeing everyone
to make sure all rules would be followed. They were standing,
three apiece, on each side of the crowd. I hesitated about join-
ing the group, but my mother shoved me in their direction.
One of the nuns looked at me and raised an eyebrow when
she saw me without a godfather. I went to stand at the rear
of the line by myself. The Bishop, dressed in his resplendent
surplice, came out through the front door from inside the
church and stopped at the top of the stairs. He blessed us all.
Father Zavala came out and stood a step behind him and to
his right. Father Zavala looked somewhat more refreshed
than he did Friday night. I could see he wanted to know
where my godfather was. He kept raising and lowering his
heavy eyebrows at me. How could I have answered? The
Bishop gave a short talk on how the Sacraments would be
conducted. Confirmation would go on first, before the regular
Sunday Mass. First Communion would take place during the
Mass at the normal time.

I looked around to see if my godfather was seen approaching. My mother and father were anxiously walking about,
going across the street to the park, looking for any signs of

José. My grandmother stood with her arms folded. Juan, Matías, Cota, Maggie, Francis, and Sylvia were all giggling to see me standing by myself, like a fool.

The Bishop continued. We were to receive Communion before the rest of the congregation. He had us form two lines, the children in one file on his right, the godparents in another on his left. The parents began to walk in. My family was standing by the side on the steps looking around, still hopeful my godfather would arrive. The procession began, the Bishop standing at the top of the stairs smiling. He was squeezing the nose of each child as they went by. When he saw that I was alone he stopped me and asked, "Who is the godfather for this child?"

Father Zavala was about to intervene.

"I am," I heard the familiar voice. It was Matías, who wasn't scared of the devil.

"And you are qualified to be a godfather?" the Bishop asked him as Matías, dressed in old trousers and a ragged shirt, went over and stood by me.

"Yes, I am," he replied.

"Yes, he is," my family agreed.

The Bishop looked at Father Zavala for an explanation. "What do you say to this?" he asked Father Zavala.

Father Zavala grabbed Matías by the ears, twisted them and said, "He is as qualified as anyone here. I know the child."

"And," the Bishop asked Matías, remaining unconvinced, "you went to Confession last night?"

"Yes, I did," he lied.

All of us, including Father Zavala, knew it was not a complete lie. Hadn't he gone to confession on Friday? What was one day? Well, it was quite a bit. We had stolen oranges from the Luby's orchard Friday night after Confession. We had stolen a chicken at the creek on Saturday, and we had eaten it in the cave. We had knocked on an old lady's door several times and hid while she wondered if she were going insane, hearing knocking when she could not find anyone at the door. Juanita, the lady who had the grocery store in the front room of her house, had paid us deposits on her own bottles, the ones we had stolen from her front porch. Juan, Matías, my brother and I had gone to sit at the back of the movie house Saturday morning while they were showing Gene Autry and we had urinated on the slanted floor and had watched the reaction of the barefooted children up front when they began to notice their feet awash in urine.

I was all right as far as sinning went. I had confessed most of my sins Saturday night. The only thing I did not confess to Father Zavala was having bad thoughts about my godfather. I hated him, and I prayed my parents never died while he was alive. Naively, I thought I would have to go live with his family. He had an awful wife and a son who never went out and played. I should have known my grandmother would have killed anyone trying to take anyone of us away from her. After Confession my mother had taken me directly from the church and put me to bed. The only sin I had was calling Juan and Matías a bad word this morning.

"And you swear by Almighty God that you have fasted?" the Bishop asked Matías.

"Yes, I have," Matías lied some more.

"And," he kept on, "you are in a state of grace?"

"I am," Matías replied. And in his heart he thought he was. Matías always believed he was better than the priests.

The Bishop placed his hand on my head, and I felt the weight of his ring. He asked, "Has your godfather gone to Confession and fasted? Is he in a state of grace?"

I had to swallow hard but I said, "Yes, he is."

That lie was a venial sin, I thought quickly, a ticket to purgatory. Someone would have to pray for me to make it up to Heaven. Moreover, not being in a state of grace, my Confirmation and Communion would not take.

Matías should have gotten an award for lying. He had not fasted. That morning, while he was making fun of me, he had been eating eggs and chorizo with tortillas and a giant cup of coffee.

My mother was about to say something to the Bishop, confess Matías had eaten, when my grandmother stopped her. My father was not paying attention. He was craning his neck looking for my lost godfather.

The Bishop looked at Father Zavala, and Father Zavala nodded. The Bishop squeezed my nose as I walked by, my godfather Matías at my side.

As we walked down the aisle to our waiting seats, Matías whispered to me, "If you say anything to the Bishop about me, I'm going to tell him you cursed this morning. Then I'll kill you." Then he let out the stinkiest burp, full of garlic, vinegar, pork meat, chili peppers, and cumin.

I wasn't going to rat on Matías. I wanted to get the Confirmation and Communion out of the way.

The Bishop did slap me hard, but my head did not feel like it was fifty feet wide. As a matter of fact, I had gotten hit a lot harder during my boxing career. He asked my name and whether I loved God. I told him my name and that I loved God a lot. Matías rolled his eyes, trying to insult me, and in doing so God punished him. He made Matías burp in front of the Bishop. It took several seconds for the stench to reach the Bishop. When it did, the Bishop took two steps back and so did my brother who was standing by the side of the Bishop holding a tin of holy ashes. My brother was making a face. Father Zavala caught the smell and moved out of the way quickly. The Bishop waved his hand in front of his nose to clear the air of the regurgitated spices. He could not fathom what the smell was. He looked down at the floor, around to the back toward the altar. Perhaps he thought some strange object had caught fire from the candles, or some strange animal had messed on the floor. Matías quickly cast his eyes on Father Zavala and shook his head, throwing the blame on the old man. The Bishop, catching Matías' stare, glared at Father Zavala and then frowned. He had identified the odor. He hated chorizo and the gases it caused. Even the priest had eaten sausage before Communion. What could he expect of the congregation?

The smell dissipated into the air in the church, diluted, and was gone. The Bishop recovered enough to continue with me. He didn't remember. Had I said I loved God? Yes. I did love God a lot. Matías didn't roll his eyes this time. I volunteered knowing the ten Commandments and all the Mysteries of the Rosary, but the Bishop only smiled at me. He did not want to hear that much from any child. And besides, I was the last one, and he didn't want to be around Father Zavala when he burped again. Matías pinched me and whispered for me to shut up.

When the ceremonies were over, we were walking home when Father Zavala came out from the garage behind the rectory. He was in a hurry to meet us.

"I don't know about this," he said, shaking his head. "The poor child may not have been confirmed for all we know. And then the question of the First Communion." He looked at Matías. "Was that chorizo you ate this morning?" he asked. "It nearly turned my stomach when I smelled your burp."

"That's my fault," my grandmother said to the good priest. "The chorizo that I made this time, I overdid the vinegar."

"We'll just leave everything up to God," my mother said.

"Yes," Father Zavala concurred. "If he can unravel all of this."

My grandmother said, "He's going to grow up fine. You just wait and see."

We had a small celebration at home. We ate a good meal and then ate cake which my mother had baked. Afterwards, my father went back to bed. We were laughing at what Matías had done when the original godfather drove in. He got off the car very slowly, leaving the car door open. He was drunk. He was dressed in his new suit and shoes and white socks. His trousers were twisted over to one side and his necktie was loose. He staggered toward the house. My grandmother and mother were watching him, cursing him under their breath. He came up the stairs, almost falling backwards twice. He knocked on the door, and when my grandmother asked him what he wanted, he said he had come to take me to Confirmation.

My grandmother and my mother would have none of him. He was, according to what my grandmother told him, a man of little worth. Not a man at all. More like a rat. "A rat never keeps its word."

The man reeled with each insult. He tried to focus his wondering eyes on my grandmother as she blasted him. Then she ran him off, told him if he ever set foot on her yard again she would personally whip him with the broom. He weaved off to his car, wondering why the two women were so angry with him.

"I'm glad I'm not going to be the child's godfather," we heard him say.

It had not made any difference. He had not been to Confession on Saturday either and surely he had not kept his fast. I was happy he hadn't showed up. I was afraid I would have to go live with him if my parents died. How could I have lived without Juan, Matías, Cota, Maggie, Francis, Richard and Sylvia?

For Confession the next time, Matías was given fifty Our Fathers, fifty Acts of Contrition, fifty Hail Marys and was made to go around the Stations of the Cross ten times.

I'm not going to tell you what he called Father Zavala after he came out of the church, but my grandmother prayed for Father Zavala that night.

Aunt Pepa

We were out in the yard in the middle of the morning playing marbles. We played a game called *canicas* in which each of us placed an equal amount of marbles inside a circle on the flattest dirt we could find. To start the game, we would draw a line about ten feet from the circle and stand behind it. Each, from oldest to youngest, would shoot our marble toward the ring. If one was lucky or good at it, it was possible from that long distance to hit a marble inside the ring and knock it out. After the first shoot, we aimed from where we lay at the marbles in the ring. Whoever knocked a marble out of the ring would pocket that marble and continue until he missed. The game ended when there were no marbles left inside the ring. Whoever knocked the most marbles out of the ring and pocketed them was the winner. I can tell you that being the smallest offered me no chance of winning. The game of *canicas* required a lot of time to master. It wasn't like baseball or boxing. Juan and Matías could knock two marbles out of the ring at the same time, like billiards, and leave their own shooting marble in position inside the ring ready for the next shot.

We were in the middle of the game when we saw Pepa running toward us through the yard next door. When she came to the fence, she climbed it light as a feather. She carried her lantern with her and it got caught at the top of the fence. She had to climb the fence again to free the lantern. She was in a hurry. She came over to us and asked me why I hadn't been to see her. I had seen her the day before. As usual, in her imagination her dead children had been there the day before and her dead husband was coming to visit her.

I did not want to walk around with Pepa anymore. She would take me around town all day long asking me all kinds of questions about the town as though she had never lived in it before. Who's house was that? I would have to tell her every day. Every day was the same. Was that the depot? No, it wasn't. Were those children her children? Was that man on horseback her husband coming to see her?

It had been all right when I was a child for her to take care of me, but now I was getting older. I did not want to walk around town with Mercé either. Juan, Matías, Cota, Frances, Maggie, and my brother and sister were beginning to make fun of me. They were saying I was crazy like them.

My mother had walked across to visit my grandmother in the kitchen of her house. Pepa stayed with us for a while, walking around talking to herself and stepping on the marbles inside the ring. Finally, I led her toward the kitchen door where she peeked through the screen and called out for my grandmother. My grandmother was not too happy to see her either. She had been there every day that week, interfering with the daily chores, asking her questions, denying she was insane. And then, after she had eaten and stayed for the nightly talks, someone had to take her back home to make sure she didn't come back. I was the one who had to take her home to be sure she got in bed, but she had already forgotten.

Her reason for being here this morning was to convince my mother and grandmother that I should live with her. She needed a companion. She was scared at night. Seeing ghosts was beginning to bother her. The creaky noises from the old house were scaring her. The voices were getting louder. The coyotes in the woods next to the house were getting closer. She was afraid they might come into the house. The drought had made them come closer, looking for food and water.

"There are no coyotes there," my grandmother said. "You're lying."

"I am not," Pepa answered. "The coyotes are there every night. I can hear them."

"It's all in your mind," my mother explained. "It's just a small patch of mesquite. There are no coyotes there."

"I am not crazy," Pepa said.

"Yes, you are," my grandmother said.

"No, I'm not," Pepa insisted.

"You can't take him," we heard my mother say.

Pepa began her murmuring as she did when she could not get her way. We could hear my grandmother consoling her. Soon my grandmother was agreeing with Pepa.

"What would it cost the child to go sleep with Pepa?" she was asking of my mother.

"Pepa is crazy," my mother replied. "That's a good enough reason."

Pepa said, "I'm not crazy. Am I crazy, María?"

My grandmother ignored the question. By now we had quit the game of marbles Pepa had ruined and were sitting on the porch by the kitchen door listening to the conversation.

"Do you want some coffee?" my grandmother asked her.

We heard Pepa place the lantern on top of the table and slide the chair against the floor to sit down.

"If you say you're not crazy, why do you carry that lantern around?" my grandmother asked.

"To see when they come," Pepa replied.

We could tell from the conversation that I was going to have to go sleep with Pepa. Everyone knew I didn't want to go with her. I didn't want to seem ungrateful, but I didn't want to go. She smelled so much of urine. And I didn't want to appear as though I didn't like her. I did. We had spent many a night together.

There were times when we would lay in bed and she would be very lucid. She told me stories of her childhood, beautiful little things that made her cry. Since early childhood, she could hear voices from everywhere—from the heavens, the trees, the grass, the leaves as they fell. Everything spoke to her. She could see apparitions in every direction—in front of her, to her sides, behind, underneath, above. She could see angels, people, animals. But she thought everyone else did, too. She never could play with a toy without giving it a name. She regarded everything as alive and having feelings. Therefore, she could never sell or get rid of anything she possessed. For instance, the lantern she carried once belonged to her mother.

As a young girl, Pepa enjoyed going to the Saturday night dances. She loved to polka and could dance the schottische and the waltz. Often, she was chosen the queen of the dance. She was so light on her feet that men stood in line to dance with her. During one Saturday night dance, she had picked up so much dust her petticoats had to be changed and her feet washed three times, she used to say. Pepa could sing, but, because she was raised with so much modesty, she never allowed anyone to hear her.

As a wife, she had baked the best bread anyone had ever tasted, Pepa would brag. She would then go into the recipe. Of course, since she wasn't baking anything by that time, all I could ever do was imagine what her bread tasted like. Salty, but not too salty. With plenty of lard and pork skins, bread which would last for days in her husband's saddle-bag. She spoke of embroidering large quilts. Those were other times, she would say when she finished. "I wish you had been there to see me," she would say as I fell asleep.

And then came the tragedies. Her first child died while she lived with her husband on a desolate ranch. She had been alone. Her husband was away for several days tending to the *patrón's* cattle. She was washing clothes by hand at the windmill. The child was asleep in its crib inside the house. She came in and checked on the baby. The child was dead in the crib. Quickly, she picked up the baby and ran with it, hoping to find someone who could help her. She ran for miles through the brush. Nightfall came and found her running on a country road. She was picked up by a family on a wagon. Her clothes were tattered; her body had gotten ripped by the brush. She had run at least ten miles with the dead child, hearing all the voices, seeing all the ghosts.

Pepa was never well afterward. She had two more sons and she lost both of them and her husband all in one year. That was enough to push her over the edge. She became a recluse, looking out at the small world through the cracks in the shutters, afraid she might die if she came out into the sunlight. She stayed in her house during the day, going out at night with her lantern to search for her children and husband in the mesquite by her house.

Then she gradually began to emerge at daybreak, to chop wood for the stove or to go into town for what little groceries she could afford. But always with the lantern in her hand.

"I'm giving him my pillow when I die," Pepa said, as though that was incentive enough for me to go sleep at her house.

We were laughing outside the door. No one wanted her stinking pillow.

"See," my grandmother said to my mother, "she might be crazy, but her heart is in the right place. Let him go. Pepa needs someone."

We did not hear my mother answer. We were already on the way to the creek. I was to hide in the cave for as long as it took. The others were to tell my mother and grandmother that I had run away forever. When Pepa's idea wore off, I would come back.

When my father came in from work, he went to the creek and took me back, straight to Pepa's. She was sitting on the porch in her rocking chair, very at ease, waiting for me. I got out of the car and walked slowly to her. She was smiling. Behind me, I heard my father drive off.

"Where have you been?" Pepa asked.

"Hiding at the creek," I said.

"I was waiting for you so we could have supper," she said, and got up and went inside.

I followed her in and went and sat at the small table. She opened her armoire, the wooden one with the perforated tin doors, and took out a tin can and a bottle of milk. She came over to the table, and using her fingertips, opened the can with much difficulty. From inside the container she counted out ten saltine crackers for me and five for her. She poured a small glass of milk for me and one for herself and sat down. We ate quietly. I was thinking that at home everyone was eating stewed meat with potatoes and rice and refried beans with hot tortillas and coffee.

After the meal, she cleaned the crumbs off the table and prepared for bed. I said I would sleep in my clothes. That way I would be up and ready to go back home as soon as I awoke.

"And you're not staying for breakfast?" she asked me. I could tell her feelings were hurt. "You always liked to eat breakfast with me before."

"I meant that I would go home after I ate breakfast," I replied. We were going to eat the same thing.

That night as we lay in bed she recounted her husband's story, a story I had heard many times. She told the story not to speak of his death, but to prove he was still alive. I wasn't prepared to go to sleep, early as it was. I was used to going to bed at midnight after hearing all the stories on my grandmother's porch and then exhausting myself playing whatever games the older ones wanted to play.

The truth was that José, her husband, had been away for several days working cattle, sleeping on the ground, and eating on the run. No one knew exactly what happened, but somehow the horse stumbled at the edge of a ravine. In his fall, the animal rolled all the way down to the bottom, crushing José several times as the horse rolled. He died alone, his horse standing over him. He must have suffered a great deal. He could have lived two, three days in a lot of pain, or died instantly. No one knew for sure. One day the horse without the rider appeared, sweaty, tired and thirsty. The search began for José.

I was lying very still next to Pepa, the sheet covering me up to my neck. Only my eyes moved to look at her. Her hands were clasped at her chest.

"He really didn't die," she said. "I'm going to tell you something I've never told anyone before," she continued. "When they told me that José was found dead, I could not believe it. He didn't die. My sons didn't die. José is alive and he had my two sons with him. They are alive. But they like to hide from me. They think I like to play games. But I became so angry with the horse that I went out to the horse pen to look for him after everyone had gone. There he was, standing alone in the dark. I had the whip that José had made, and I went into the pen and I whipped the horse until I could not stand anymore. The next morning I could not move my arm."

As soon as it was dark I could hear Juan, Matías, Cota, Maggie, Frances, Richard and Sylvia out in the woods by the house making yelping noises like a pack of coyotes. It was their way of making fun of me. They were having a great time. Their bellies were full.

"I'm scared. The coyotes are coming into town," Pepa said when she heard them. "That's the sign of a drought."

Then she gave me her pillow to use. I didn't want it. It smelled of urine, like the rest of her. But she insisted. I might as well get used to it. It was going to be mine after she died.

She began to twiddle her thumbs constantly. She wanted me to go to sleep because the next day after breakfast we were going to go look for them. We might see them tomorrow, she said.

After a few weeks, she forgot to take me with her, and since an insane person considers one miss as good as a tradition, she forgot about needing me for the time being. To be safe, I avoided her for a few months.

That was to be the last time I slept with her. I was eight then. I did go and do chores for her, but she slept alone.

Pepa lived a long time, long enough for me to suffer the jokes about her pillow, my inheritance. By the time she died, the pillow was a flat, thin rectangle of shredded cotton, smelling more of urine than ever before. After the funeral, Juan cut the pillow open because he felt Pepa might have left some money for me for all the chores I had done. All we found as we tore into the innards of the pillow was the cotton, soaked with the urine of so many years.

I did get to keep the lantern.

Harry

The oil boom came to predominantly Mexican South Texas in the forties. Along with the boom came an influx of Anglos to work the oil fields. This invasion of strangers was a new experience for us. We had never been directly exposed to Anglo culture. Their way of living was completely alien to us. Never had we seen so much food eaten and thrown away; so many women smoking and drinking alongside their men, kissing their husbands in the mouth passionately in front of the children; dogs and cats living inside the house. We had never seen so many refrigerators, so much candy, ice-cream bought by the gallon, soda-pop by the case; young girls showing off their legs, their panties, their intimate parts; young children smoking; mistresses and their children living with men for a while, moving on to live with someone else; mothers running around in negligee all day long offering their children and us soda-pop and candy for lunch and dinner, their large breasts barely hidden, their projectile-shaped nipples pointing at us at the table, making us feel guilty just by eating; cakes with frosting that smeared over into our noses; women cursing for real, not the funny cursing of my grandmother, but the heavy type that you only heard from men in the streets.

We had always thought that women were supposed to stay at home while the men went out and got drunk. Never in our little town had anyone ever seen a lady in a restaurant. Restaurants were for men and prostitutes. Women were supposed to work at home, carry on with other women. Women were not supposed to go out except to church and once in a while to the movies.

146

These new women that moved in went to restaurants and sat with the men and drank beer in the beer halls.

They were a happy people. Nothing seemed to bother them. Money flowed from them like water out of a pitcher. They were kindhearted and wanted to help everyone. They took to us a lot easier than we took to them.

In contrast, we were happy, but we worried about where the next dime would come from, about not spending money on anything foolish, about when the next disaster was coming. Because Mexicans are worriers. Even when things are going his way, a Mexican worries. He worries that things are going his way. He worries because God is being so good to him. Also, we love to suffer. Everything enjoyable, we have been taught, is bad.

The Anglos that came to live with us believed everything enjoyable was good. But we had been taught that we should try to go to Heaven. The Anglos were trying to go wherever they pleased, Heaven included.

Our two philosophies were so opposed that we were astounded God did not strike them dead for their ways. They never confessed their sins, never went to Mass!

These hordes needed places to rent. There was money to be made in renting out homes. We had not known that my grandmother had thought about renting her house, but apparently she had. One day she told our mother she had decided to rent it. That caused an argument which lasted for days, followed by a silence between the two parties lasting several more days.

My grandmother had thought it out without consulting our mother. My grandfather was in San Antonio working at the liquor store. She and the children—Juan, Matías, Cota, Maggie, and Frances—could live in the shed in the back yard.

"There's not enough room in the shed," my mother argued.

"We'll add to the shed then," my grandmother said.

"With what money?" my mother inquired.

"You'll see," my grandmother answered.

She asked us to go get Miguel Canchola, one of the town carpenters. We ran to the north side of town, at least six blocks past the courthouse, to where the carpenter lived, and we found him drunk, sitting outside in a rocking chair. We

woke him up and brought him home. My grandmother
explained what she wanted.

"Two rooms and a kitchen," she said.

Miguel Canchola stepped back from the shed and stuck
up his thumb an arm's length from his face. He mumbled
some figures to himself as he measured out the plan.

"It can be done," he said. "And how am I to be paid?"

"I am a woman of my word," my grandmother replied. "As
the rent from the big house comes in, I'll pay you."

"I've known you forever," Miguel uttered, "and I know you
would rather starve than not pay your debts."

The next day he and his son arrived ready for work with
their tools inside a wheelbarrow. We helped him carry the
materials from the lumberyard to the house. In the middle of
the morning and the afternoon, my grandmother brought out
coffee and Mexican pastries. We drank and ate as though we
were part of the crew. We were fascinated with Miguel
Canchola. He measured approximate lengths through the tri-
angulation of his thumb and his eye at the distance of his
extended arm. For more accurate measurements, he used a
cloth tape with faded numbers which he carried inside his
pocket. In no time, he was done. It was not very straight, but
he was done. He even added a lopsided porch to the front of
the shed.

It didn't take long for the word to get around. One morning a car drove up to our grandmother's house loaded with
red-headed children. We went over to see who it was. The
woman driving got out and greeted us warmly. We could tell
she was a good woman, slightly wild like the rest of them, but
good-hearted. She was tall, in white shorts and a red midriff,
with long legs, blond hair with black roots, and a raspy voice.
On her feet she wore brightly colored red sandals. (If my
mother had dressed like this woman, my father would have
killed her and we would have had to look for her in pieces.)
Her hair was a mess after driving around in the heat with
the windows down. She was smoking, holding the cigarette
daintily between her index and middle fingers. On both
hands, the tips of their fingers were stained brown. She held
the cigarette away from her, so the smoke would not float her
way. She closed one eye that was full of smoke. With the
other hand she pressed her fingers into her forehead as if she
had a headache.

This lady, who came into our lives that day, was Lola Davis, one-quarter Choctaw, one-quarter Kiowa, and one-half tiger from Oklahoma.

"Goddamit," she said in her heavy voice. She rubbed the eye, bent down to take care of it, and said, "Harry, for Christ's sake, get out of the car and help me, will you? Jesus Christ."

Harry, a lean, red-headed young boy, came out of the car to help his mother. Except for his red hair, he was completely white underneath the freckles that covered him from head to toe, like a mottled goat. She handed him the cigarette. "Here," she said, "you smoke the rest of this sumbitch. I got somethin' in my eye." Harry hadn't looked at us yet. He was trying to help his mother straighten out. She finally did and leaned on the fender of the car. "Goddam," she said out loud. "Gettin' to where I can't smoke a cigarette without somethin' bad happenin' to me." To Harry she said, remembering his problems, "Don't smoke too much of that. You know the doctor don't want you smokin' no more. Throw it away. Now throw it away, Harry."

Harry took one short puff in a hurry, inhaling the smoke deeply. He thought about the pleasure the cigarette in his hand could give him, and he took another quick drag. Then he threw the cigarette away where it rolled in the dust.

Inside the car were two girls. They were looking out and giggling, eating some type of cookies we had never seen before, dark chocolate with something white and soft in the middle. Their mouths were smeared with chocolate.

"You girls git out," Lola said, looking into the car and waving her hand. "Git. Git out."

We watched the girls get out, two red-headed girls wearing white shorts and cute little white leather thongs that showed their delicately painted toes. They had more color than Harry. They were very white with bright red cheeks and blue eyes, deep colored, like marbles. Both girls seemed to be transparent in the sun. They were wearing white T-shirts that clung to their tiny developing breasts and over-sized projecting nipples. They lined up by the front fender next to Lola, who was now standing up but still rubbing her eye.

Juan and Matías almost died when they saw the girls. Visions danced in their heads. They could see themselves playing with them. Cota and Maggie and Frances and Sylvia and Richard and I couldn't play with the girls if they played with them. That was for sure. For sure we would be in the way. They would let Harry play with us. They could play with these girls under the house where it was cool and where no one could see them. They could go over to the creek and spend the day inside the cave, maybe do some kissing and who knew what else. Maybe they could take food and cook it and play like they were married. Maybe they could go in the water in the creek and see what their breasts looked like under their wet T-shirts. Maybe they could get the girls to show them their breasts. Juan and Matías were sure they could. They could steal cigarettes and give them to the girls, and then the girls would show them everything. But they had cigarettes. Well then, they could steal candy, maybe that would do it. But the girls had candy. Juan and Matías could steal some of those cookies the girls were eating, if they could find out where the girls got them. It didn't make any difference. Juan and Matías would ask them what they wanted, what they wanted more than anything else. Then that would do it.

Lola asked for our grandmother, who was inside the house cooking another meal. My grandmother had heard the car and the commotion that Lola had made when the cinder got in her eye.

"Goddam eye won't stop hurtin'," she said to all of us. "Look into it and see." She held the eye open for Harry to inspect. The young boy looked into his mother's eye against the sunlight and said he couldn't see anything. By this time the giggling girls had gone over to peer into Lola's eye.

"It's fine," Harry said, walking away from her to go to the front of the car. He leaned against the radiator. He took out some candy from inside his pocket, opened it, and began to eat.

"You can never see anythin'," his mother complained. "And don't eat too much candy 'cause the doctor says that your lungs are no good. You know that. Chocolate is bad for you." Then she looked at us watching Harry eat his candy and said to him, "You ought to share with these children. Harry, you and the girls go and play with them," she said, meaning us. Harry and the girls looked the other way and stayed their ground.

We watched as Harry ignored his mother and finished tearing the cover off the candy. He ate what was left in two bites just to aggravate her.

Our grandmother was standing on the porch. She had the broom in her hand to help her walk down the steps. Lola saw her and smiled. She walked over and held out her hand to help our grandmother step down.

Our grandmother understood enough English to know Lola wanted to rent the house. My mother came out from next door. She interpreted anyway. Our grandmother was having second thoughts about renting. It just wasn't the Mexican way to rent your house. My mother reminded her that she had told her so. Our grandmother ignored my mother and kept on, almost weeping. A house is a precious thing, the most memorable part of your life. In a house, she said, things happen to a family that only the four walls know. Those were the secrets of a house, secrets which belong to the family for all eternity.

Lola meant well, but she was in a hurry to find a place. She said to my mother, "Well, tell her to think fast 'cause I've got a shitload of furniture and all my other shit in a truck in Alice, and I need to get it unloaded pretty damn pronto."

Our grandmother needed more time. Lola said sure, and she went and sat inside the car while Harry and the girls stayed outside with us. Lola lit a cigarette. From the car Lola said, smoke coming out of her mouth, "When I finish this damn cigarette, I need an answer."

While Lola smoked her cigarette, our grandmother stood on the porch wringing her hands, wondering what she should do. Lola finished her cigarette and came out of the car.

"What's it to be?" she asked.

Our grandmother agreed to rent the house. We were so happy. We were going to have someone else to play with. Harry became more interested in us. He smiled at us and then looked around the yard to see how he liked it. The two young girls stayed around the car, giggling, following the shade. Our grandmother brought out some water, and the girls and Lola had some. Lola called Harry over and gave him some water.

Then after Harry had his water, she said, "Here, so you don't get sick." She took some of the water and poured it in her hand and smeared it on Harry's forehead. "You need to cool off," she told him.

She looked at him with a lot of love and smiled. Harry turned red. Lola realized she had embarrassed Harry in front of us. This being his first time around us, she did not want us to think Harry was easy to push around. She felt badly about it and offered him a cigarette. Harry took it with a tough, manly gesture and stuck it on the side of his mouth. She lit it for him and Harry leaned against the fender and smoked. We were fascinated to see Harry smoking, blowing smoke high over his head. Nothing was happening to him. The gods were not parting the skies. If we had lit a cigarette in front of my mother, we would have been injured. We had seen grown men and women with families who did not smoke in front of their parents.

Lola hugged us all, told us she had to leave for Alice to go get her "shit." She got Harry and the girls into the car and backed it up.

At the entrance to the driveway, our grandmother had an old concrete pot where she planted portulaca, that being the only flowering plant which survived the heat and droughts of South Texas. Lola backed straight into the pot, toppled it over, and crushed it. She got out, said some more goddamits, and apologized to our grandmother. Our grandmother went over and collected the pieces and placed them off to one side. Lola said she would pay for the damage and took out a five-dollar bill, a fortune to us. Our grandmother refused. Lola said she would make it up to her.

Our grandmother spent a good deal of time trying to put the broken pieces together, but in the end she couldn't and we didn't want to help her. We were too excited about the family moving in.

That afternoon, early, the truck arrived with the furniture and several men. They began to empty my grandmother's house. At the same time, my grandmother was sitting on the porch of the little house at the rear, crying. Each sob was an exaggeration, so heartfelt and sorrowful. She had done the unspeakable, allowing other people to live in her house, the house her mother had willed to her. She had not only betrayed her beloved mother, she had betrayed all her ancestors. My mother was yelling from across the yard that that was what she got for not paying attention to her.

The men moving the furniture kept wondering what all the crying and the shouting was about. They excused themselves every time they passed by with my grandmother's furniture, looking down gravely at her. At first they asked if someone had died, and she replied as best she could through the tears that it might as well have been the case. Her heart had been ripped out of her chest. My grandmother would look up at them from her chair, her eyes swollen from crying, looking upward like the Virgin Mary.

Then came Lola in her car loaded with so many things that we could hardly see her and the children. She ran out, opened the trunk, and with a great effort she and Harry lifted a concrete pot out. She had bought my grandmother a new one in Alice, bigger one than the original. She had it potted with twice as much portulaca, to hell with the cost. She and Harry carried the large pot to where the other had been and set it down. Lola inspected it from different angles, pointing at it with her cigarette finger as Harry readjusted the setting. When she was satisfied, she threw the cigarette down and Harry picked it up. They came over to where my grandmother sat crying.

"I promise you, María," she said, as she approached, "that I will never run over another pot again. And if I do, I'll buy you another one. A bigger one." As soon as she got to the porch, she noticed the tears. "Why in the world are you cryin'?" she asked, coming up to the porch and sitting down by my grandmother. She put her cigarette arm around my grandmother.

We explained that my grandmother felt very badly about leaving her house. Lola offered to leave. "I can find any old house to live in," she said. "Nothin' is forever, María." But my grandmother told her to stay. She would be all right in a few days.

"*Es que me duele mucho*," our grandmother complained, squeezing her heart.

We looked around for the girls and could not see them. We went over and made friends with Harry, and then Juan and Matías asked in a roundabout way about the girls. Harry said that those were his cousins from Alice and not his sisters. What a disappointment for Juan and Matías. They had that look about them for awhile, as if they had been shown something good to eat and then had it snatched from their plates.

The house smelled different once Lola moved in. She smoked constantly and was always sipping out of a glass of clear alcohol. It was gin, but we didn't know it. She loaded the kitchen and the refrigerator with groceries. So the old house lost its quaint mustiness and took on the smell of tobacco, alcohol, and groceries—bread, ice-cream, bananas, grapes, oranges, lemons, plums. Yes, plums!

We found out Lola wasn't married. Her man drove to and from the oil fields every day. His name was Jack. He was a big red-headed man, heavy in every way. He had huge arms, a huge chest and was short-legged. He spoke rough and lived rough. No one ever crossed him, not in the oil fields or any- where else. He didn't like children to be around him, Harry included, except when he was drunk. And then he would be hard to get away from. He loved to squeeze you, rub your head with his knuckles, laughing all the time. Then he would turn serious and look at Lola like she had done something wrong to him. These abrupt changes in mood bothered us. It was the alcohol working on him.

When Jack got drunk, Lola would try to keep Harry out, which was all right with Harry. Harry would rather get away from the man. When that happened, Harry came to sleep with us.

This was when we had taken to sleeping at my Mercé's house just for the fun of it. There were no lights except a lantern, and all of us would sleep in the same room, some in the old iron bed with the iron springs, some on quilts strewn on the floor. We would lay awake looking at the shadows cast on the wall by the lapping flame from the lantern, dancing shadows that eerily brought ghosts to mind. Juan and Matías and Cota and Maggie and Frances would tell stories, try to get everyone scared so we wouldn't go to the toilet outside. How many people had died in that room, someone asked, and our eyes got big, our hearts began to pound.

Juan told the story of how my grandmother's sister had died in that room on that same bed one night when it was storming. He made noises like thunder in the distance, like rain on the tin roof. Matías howled like a coyote. Maggie answered him. My grandmother's sister had died in a fit. No one knew of a cure for epilepsy then. Juan told about when she died. How the men had to hold her down to keep her from floating to the top of the rafters.

Cota began the story of the snake that lived under the house. The snake milked a young mother's breasts at night while she slept in that same bed, robbing milk from the baby. The baby was starving to death. The mother was slowly losing all her strength. The husband stayed up one night to pray for his wife and child. Unseen to him, while he was dozing, the snake crawled in through the window. Suddenly the husband awoke and noticed the movement on the floor across the bed. The snake lifted its head above the mattress, looked around with its wicked empty stare, flicked its tongue to seek the warmth of the breast, and then started to slither into the bed with the woman. The husband watched in awe as the snake attached its hungry mouth to the woman's breast and began to milk her. At the same time, the snake wiggled its tail in front of the child's mouth. The husband stood in horror as the child, barely awake, grasped the tail with his little fingers and stuck the tail into his mouth. The child began to suck the snake's tail placidly. The snake sucked and engorged itself with the mother's milk. The husband was frantic, looking for something to kill the snake. He found the shotgun behind the kitchen door. Quickly he ran to his wife and child, wrapped the snake around his arm and tugged until he was able to pull it off the nipple. The snake whipped around, slashing into the man's skin, and began to wrap itself around the man. Desperate, he threw down the shotgun and untangled himself from the snake. When he was free of the snake, he threw the snake against the wall. The snake hit the wall and stuck there, forming a perfect S. Then it began to crawl to the floor where it placed its tail in its mouth and made itself into a hoop, spinning around the room, looking for an escape. The husband began to shoot in the semidarkness. Faster and faster the snake circled the room, inching its way toward the husband with every circle that it made. The unsatisfied baby began to cry. The young mother awakened. At first she noticed the milk oozing out of her nipple, and then she saw the snake, its tail in its mouth, formed into a large hoop, rolling around the room. She yelled for her husband. The husband fired again. The snake found a way out through the window, the same window that we were sleeping

under. Tragically, the shot sprayed past the snake, hitting
the baby and the wife. It killed the baby.

It had all happened in that room. The snake still came by
after all these years, looking for milk. Once a snake tastes
human milk it will always seek out a woman asleep. This was
the same snake, must have been sixty, seventy years old. It
still lived under Mercé's house. It was the dreaded *alicante*,
the hoop snake that only a few elders had ever seen, the
snake they delighted telling us about. Harry had never heard
of the *alicante*. It surprised us how ignorant Harry was about
these animals.

Mercé had spoken to a ghost in that same room, a Civil
War soldier wearing a uniform with gold buttons.

Harry was speechless. We could hear him moving around
on the iron springs, adjusting his body to the pain of sleeping
on the springs with only a quilt underneath him. He was
scared from the stories and scared at his own ignorance about
the *alicante*.

After we had quieted down and fallen asleep, we heard
Mercé come in. We heard him stumble around drunk. He was
mumbling about something like he usually did. He went into
his room off to one side, and we heard him fall on the bed as
if he had collapsed and died. In a few moments Mercé started
one of his insane fits, and he stumbled through the darkened
house cursing. When Mercé ran by the bed, he tripped and
fell on top of Harry. Harry screamed that Mercé was going to
kill us all. We told him to shut up. Mercé was harmless. He
was just insane. Juan and Matías and Cota and Frances and
Maggie were trying to untangle Mercé from the iron springs,
but they had to wait until Mercé finished with his fit. When
he was through, we relit the lantern and checked him out. He
had scratched himself a little, but that was all. We gave
Mercé one of Harry's cigarettes and put him to bed. Then we
quieted Harry down.

After we had settled down and gone to sleep, Juan
sneaked out through the front door and came around to
scratch on the window. We awoke with the noise he was making and got up to see who it was. Juan had taken the lantern
and was standing in the dark at the back of the yard by the
outhouse, shining the light from the lantern into his face. His
face was the only thing we could see. It was a lighted and

moving head that seemed to float in the air. We ran and hid under the covers. Mercifully, Mercé was snoring in his bed.

Harry began to cry, and we felt sorry for him. He wanted to be with Lola, but his mother had gone to Alice to dance with Jack and would not come home until the early morning hours. Matías told him to be quiet. He sounded like a calf crying for its mother. Harry quit crying and lit a cigarette and he passed it around. The cigarette seemed to calm him down. He asked if the snake had been seen recently. Matías said he had seen it just a few days ago, its tail in its mouth, formed into a hoop, spinning its way across the yard. Harry sighed a lot and took several drags from his cigarette. Then he slept and began to breathe so heavily that he kept us awake.

He was an only child, sad in many ways. He had had a sister who had died in Oklahoma. We had never known anyone as frail. As we got to know him better, he became a good friend. He went to school with Juan, Matías, Cota, Maggie, and Frances. He never argued like we did. He went along with whatever we told him to do. He always had cigarettes and candy and gum. I'm sure he found us strange in a lot of ways.

He was very ignorant about animals. Once when Harry went with us to the creek, we had the misfortune of encountering a dragonfly. My brother saw it first. He pointed to it and screamed like someone had pulled out one of his fingernails. We all saw the dragonfly then, and immediately started to run for our lives. We had been taught that the dragonfly, which to us was a *chupa huesos* or "bone-sucker," sucked the marrow out of the bones. After that happened, you turned into a mass of wrinkled flesh. Death followed instantly. Harry stayed around, watching us run. He did not know the dangers of the dragonfly. He scratched his small head, wondering what we were doing. We were yelling for him to run for cover. The dragonfly was right by him, about to suck the marrow from his bones. How could we explain it to Lola when we showed up without Harry? How could we explain that Harry had died at the creek? Juan finally had the nerve to run to him, grab him, and drag him out of harm's way. He had saved Harry. To think that Harry had never been afraid of dragonflies before! We wondered out loud how he had survived all those years.

Lola insisted we call her Lola. No Mrs. This or Mrs. That.
She was not up to being a mother. Everyday she would go out
and come back with a carload of groceries. We ate at Harry's
a lot, Lola paying us off for taking care of him. She didn't
know how close to death Harry had come with the dragonfly,
and none of us ever told her.

We could hear Harry cough at night. Sometimes we had
to move so we could get away from the noise. Cota made a tea
for him one day. She called it Cough Tea. It was made of
pomegranate roots, bitter oranges, and garlic. The girls cut
up the ingredients and boiled them, and Harry drank the tea.
That night he did not cough as much or so it seemed to us. So
we made him drink the tea from then on. You could not imagine how bad he stank after drinking the tea. Lola was grate-
ful to us for preparing the tea for Harry. She had been taking
Harry to the doctor in Alice, but she was sure our remedy
was better than his. She gave us ice cream by the bowlfuls,
interrupting our play. We loved it. We couldn't help but
swing our feet contentedly off the porch while we ate our ice
cream and thought about games to play.

We could recreate cowboy movies from the opening scene
to the last. Juan, the eldest, usually gave himself the starring
role. He was Johnny Mac Brown or Hopalong Cassidy, and
then from the eldest to the lowest we were assigned our
parts. I was the youngest, so I usually played the Indian or
the bad guy or Frog or Gabby Hayes. I could do a good Gabby
Hayes at one time. Once, we got carried away and we hanged
a neighborhood boy for cattle rustling and almost killed him.
His mother came out running and screaming and took the
broom to us. She cut him off the tree. Luckily, the tips of his
toes were touching the ground and he didn't get hurt.

Harry's two cousins, the young girls, came to visit one
day. They arrived in a large car the likes of which we had
never seen. It was a long black car with two antennas, white
tires, a steering wheel covered in leather, and a brand new
sun visor. The inside was white and brown, like cowhide. The
girls stayed for the day, and Juan and Matías played with
them, trying to see if the girls would show them something.
They would catch glimpses here and there, but never anything definite, nothing they could feast their eyes on for a
while. The cousins seemed to be oblivious to what Juan and
Matías were trying to do. They played with such abandon—

raising their legs, kicking about, running with their dresses
held up against their waist—that it got Juan and Matías boiling. Never once did Harry ask them to play under the house.

The girls were a disappointment until it was time for
them to leave. Then they whined that they wanted to stay
and play under the house, but it was too late, their mother
said.

Lola and Jack never seemed to get along. One night we
had gone inside the house to get Harry's things when Jack
and Lola got into a fight. Lola must have been very drunk
because she swung at him and missed. He swung at her and
hit her between the eyes with his large fist. The force of the
blow made Lola jump up about a foot. She fell backwards on
top of the kitchen table. Her legs rebounded up toward her
head showing us that she wasn't wearing any panties under
her dress. We all looked at Harry to see if Harry had seen
what we had seen. Lola did not move. She was out, sprawled
on top of the table. Her dress remained over her head showing us her bare bottom. Jack picked her up, threw her over
his shoulder and carried her into the bathroom. He put her in
the bathtub and ran water over her. He shouted at us, and
we ran out to hide on the porch of the little house at the end
of the yard. Harry thought his mother was dead and was crying, but we told him not to cry. Lola would be all right. In the
morning she was feeling bad, had a hangover, she said. "If
fightin' don't kill you," she said, showing my grandmother the
welt between the eyes, "then gin will."

"What a people!" my grandmother said in Spanish.

The fighting would come and go. Some days Jack would
be the most gentle of men. He would take Lola dancing in
Alice. He would take her out to eat. Other times he would be
like a mad bull, knocking things around, breaking furniture,
throwing food at the walls.

One fight changed Harry's life.

This time Jack had Lola by the throat and she screamed.
She had never screamed before. We could see it angered
Harry when he heard Lola. He was playing with us, but he
was about to cry. Suddenly, he dropped his marbles and ran
in to save his mother. We were right behind him. We were
afraid Jack would kill Harry if he interfered.

Harry ran into the kitchen and saw Jack strangling Lola
on the kitchen table. He took a leap and landed on top of

Jack. He was hitting Jack with both fists, yelling at him to let his mother go. The exertion was too much. He began to cough, but he wouldn't stop. We could see him turning blue. We were around him trying to pull him away. But Jack was so powerful. We were only a slight bother to him. He was brushing us aside. His face was deep red with anger as he squeezed Lola's throat harder. Lola, like Harry, was turning blue. Harry had slipped down to Jack's feet and was holding on to his legs. In between coughs, Harry was screaming for his mother. While suffocating to death, Lola reached into the pocket of her house dress, pulled out a small .22 pistol, held it against Jack's stomach, and fired.

When Jack felt the burning shot pierce his stomach, he released Lola and looked at himself to see what had happened. He had heard the pistol go off, but could not believe Lola had shot him. Lola rolled off the table and fell to the floor, but was able to say, "I told you I would shoot you, you sumbitch."

Jack staggered back and sat down at the kitchen table.

"Why the fuck did you do that?" he asked, covering up the wound.

Lola staggered to her feet and sat down by him. She said, "Because I'm tired of all this fuckin' fightin', that's why."

Jack touched his wound and tried to laugh. He looked at Lola and shook his head as though she had disappointed him.

"You could've kicked me or done somethin' else," he said. "But not shoot me. What kind of chickenshit thing is that for a woman to do to her man?"

He took his hand off the little entry hole and peered down at it. He was not bleeding. Harry was still on the floor crying and coughing. We were standing around mesmerized. We had never seen a man shot before.

Lola said, "Goddamit, Harry, get up. You're making me nervous. Stop that coughing. And you children get out of here. There's no reason for any of you to be seein' this."

We couldn't move.

Jack asked for a drink. Lola poured him some gin. He looked at the glass and then he gave us an empty stare and drank it. He would be all right in a few moments he was saying to Lola, after he caught his breath. If he wasn't, she was going to have to drive him to the hospital in Alice.

He said, "And I'm goin' to have to miss work on account of you shootin' me."

Harry got up and came to stand with us.

"Harry," said Lola, "you and the children go out and play. Will you? Will you, please? Will you take them out of here? There's no cause for you children to be seeing this."

Jack checked the wound again, this time very delicately. It had begun to hurt.

"Why the fuck did you shoot me?" he asked again. "You could have cried out or somethin'. You know I wasn't goin' to kill you."

"You had me by the throat, goddam," said Lola. "How could I say anythin'? You're too strong. You don't realize how strong you are. You were killin' me. I just had a few more seconds to go. I told you I was goin' to arm myself. I gave you fair warnin'."

"I was just showin' you who's boss. That's all," Jack said.

He checked the wound, taking his shirt tail out. We could see the small hole right above the belly button oozing a pink fluid. Lola poured him another drink. She had forgotten about us.

He said, "And with a goddam .22. You shot me with a .22. What kind of gun is that?"

Lola said, "That's all I had."

"You got the goddam pistol from your sister in Alice. Ain't that right?"

"Who cares," said Lola. "How are you feelin'?"

He was quiet. We could tell the pain was beginning to get to him. His color had changed from a moment ago. He was paler. He began to breathe with much difficulty, making rasping sounds like Harry. Jack tried to get up, stood up part of the way, and then fell back on his chair. He slumped forward on the table, hitting his head with a loud thud. He hadn't felt a thing.

Lola killed Jack that night.

In those days, in South Texas, one could easily get away with murder and Lola did. She was indicted and jailed for a while. During her short stay, she became friends with the sheriff. The talk around town was that she was having an affair with the sheriff. We used to go visit her every day, take Harry with us to be with his mother. My grandmother fixed meals for her, and we'd run over to the jail with her meals three, four, sometimes five times a day. At night we used to play at the courthouse lawn in front of the jail so she could see Harry.

My grandmother thought Lola should have been paid for killing Jack, and so did the rest of the town.

It took one morning to pick the jury; most of the people known to Lola by then. The trial was after lunch and lasted fifteen minutes. By the time we found seats in the courtroom, the trial was over. The sheriff was the only witness for the defense. No one was going to argue with him.

Seeing his mother in jail and being tried for murder understandably affected Harry. His health deteriorated. Lola began to blame herself for Harry's bad health. Harry's cough grew worse despite our tea. He began to lose weight while we were gaining it. Lola kept taking him to the doctor in Alice. Then, when that doctor gave up, she took him to the doctor in town, but he could do no good. By then Harry did not have the strength to go to the creek. Sometimes Lola, feeling sorry for him, would ask us to take him anyway, and we would carry him to the creek. On those occasions, he got tired very easily. He could not climb the trail up to the cliff where we had our cave. He would stay at the bottom by the creek waiting for us, smoking his cigarette. Not even the dreaded dragonflies bothered him.

Lola took him once more to the doctor and brought him back and put him to bed. He grew weaker. He could not smoke.

One night he wanted to go sleep with us at Mercé's house, and we took him. We were afraid to go to sleep, afraid that he might die on us during the night. We were afraid to tell stories. Thank God Mercé came in very late and didn't have time to have an insane fit. We were relieved to find Harry was alive in the morning.

He lost more weight and finally could not get out of bed. The doctor did not know what was wrong with him. He tried everything he knew. We took him to Corpus Christi to see a specialist, and he informed Lola that there was no cure for what ailed Harry. Regardless, Lola took him and us to Corpus Christi Bay to show us how much water there was in this world. We already knew; we told Lola. Our parents used to take us often to the beach to cure whatever skin disease we had. Everyone, except Lola and Harry, knew that salt water cured ringworm.

Harry sat on the beach and played with a bit of sand without much interest. By afternoon, he had built a small house. We were running at the water's edge, afraid to go in. Our grandmother had told us that the devil lived in the sea.

We drove back tired from the beach, Harry not saying anything, not responding to Lola's questions. In Alice, Lola stopped at a restaurant, and since the restaurant did not serve Mexicans, she got off and brought us each a hamburger. We ate them in the car on the way to San Diego. That was the first time in our lives that we had eaten a hamburger. I did not want to finish mine. I wanted the hamburger to last forever.

We arrived home and we helped put Harry to bed in my grandmother's old bedroom. He stayed there for days, not able to get up except to move his legs off the bed to go to the bathroom. Lola stayed with him night and day. My grandmother started to bring food for her and Harry.

One cold Saturday afternoon, when we had come in from the movies and were recreating the movie again in our backyard, Lola called us in. We ran into the house to see what she wanted.

"Harry died," she said softly, as though she did not want to disturb him. When? Just then. Not one minute ago.

We tiptoed quietly into the room and saw him. We spoke in whispers. I swore I had seen him move, but then, after a while, I was sure that I had imagined it. He was not breathing. Except for his red-head, his little frail body was covered with a white sheet. We were afraid of him. We thought he could get up and chase us. No one cried. Lola told us Harry had been watching us play outside. She told us how much Harry and she loved us. Then she broke down and cried.

To everyone who knew her, Lola appeared to be a cold-hearted, practical woman. But Lola cried like no one would have believed. She buried Harry in San Diego, and she went to visit his grave every day she lived there.

Eventually, work became scarce in the oil patch. The major drilling and the building of derricks was over. Most of the men moved on with their families. Lola was not spared. She had been working as a waitress in Alice, but that ended. She could not find work to support herself. Like us, she was living a meager life. My grandmother would have to send food. She decided to return to Oklahoma. She could go back to work as a nurse again, what she had been doing before meeting Jack.

She left, promising my grandmother that she would send money for flowers on the anniversary of Harry's death. Every year, a few days before March 20th, the money would arrive. My grandmother and my mother would take us to the grave, and we would leave the flowers there for Harry.

That was not the end of Lola.

A few years later we were all in the kitchen talking when she drove in unannounced and very quietly, not like the Lola that we had known. My grandmother looked out the kitchen door at the old rusty car with Oklahoma license plates. It was Lola getting out. My grandmother met her on the porch and they embraced, crying their way through their memories. My mother came over, and Lola embraced her and had another good cry. She was still smoking, getting smoke into everyone's eyes. As we came out of the kitchen, she remembered Harry all over again. She embraced us, the gentle sobs starting anew. Finally, she broke down completely for a few moments. And then she recovered, apologized, and began to talk. We went inside and my grandmother served her coffee while we watched.

She had grown old so quickly. She was thin and drawn, the veins under her thin skin blue and thickened. She was subdued and remorseful, and it showed in the desperate glances she gave us. When she did look at us eye-to-eye for a few moments, it was with such a repentant stare that we all felt sorry for her. My grandmother sensed Lola's discomfort and wanted to tell her that whatever had happened had not been her fault, but she could not find the words in English. We told Lola what my grandmother was trying to say.

"Was I a good mother?" she asked finally, as if that was the question she had driven all the way from Oklahoma to ask, the question that had been gnawing at her for all these years.

My grandmother said she had been the best mother in the world. My mother agreed. Lola was glad to hear the good words about her, but she did not believe them. She had carried so heavy a guilt for so many years that she could not find peace no matter who offered it to her or how often.

She stayed with us for two days, walking slowly through the house, deep in thought, reminiscing in every room.

"This is where Harry liked to sleep," she said in my grandmother's old bedroom. She walked over to the window and placed her hand on the screen. "I remember the breeze would come in through this same window. He could see the stars at night. Do you remember," she asked us, "how you'd all like to sit in the kitchen and eat ice cream?" We remembered. We remembered all the groceries. "And Harry loved all of you so much. I never knew you had saved his life at the creek," she said. "He told me before he died." That must have been the incident with the dragonfly. Harry had finally believed us.

Each room brought memories for her. She slept in Harry's bed, stroking it before she lay down.

From the looks of her car and her clothes, we knew she had little money, but she went out and bought groceries for my grandmother. She bought her another concrete pot planted with portulaca. She had not forgotten my grandmother's generosity.

"This is for all the rent I owe you," she said.

Every day we visited Harry. We took flowers and a hoe and a rake to clean the grave site. We sat under the mesquite and drank the sodas and ate the ice cream Lola brought with her.

When it was time for her to go, she said, "Remember, María, when you were cryin' when I was movin' in? That seems like such a long time ago. Remember I told you that nothin' is forever?" She smiled and shook her head. She kept on. "I didn't think then that it would come to this. I didn't realize Harry was my life until he was gone."

Early, on the day she was leaving, my grandmother fixed a dozen potato and egg tacos for her to eat on the road. She left in tears.

She continued to send money for the flowers, and with the money she began to include a note. She was fine, had lost more weight. She worried daily about Harry's grave. How was it? We did not want to tell her that the headstone she had bought for Harry had sunk. She was with a new man, a tender man, but not a good provider. She enjoyed his company, but he was broke all the time. He was a door-to-door shoe salesman. She did not know why, but she had never been able to attract a good man. Her health was excellent. She had tried to stop smoking but couldn't. It had made her go Indian-crazy like she had with Jack. She had a new job. The old hospital had closed, and she was now commuting ten miles to a new hospital. How was Harry? Had we cleaned the grave?

Then, one year, she disappeared. We did not hear from her. My grandmother and my mother worried about her. They wrote letters, but never received an answer. Whether she had died or whether the pain of remembering Harry every year became too much, we did not know. She might have finally let go after all those years. What we wanted her to know was that we still kept the grave clean, that we had so many relatives buried at the cemetery that taking care of Harry was no problem at all.

We never heard from her again.

The Haircut

As usual, on Friday night we were waiting for my grandfather to drive in from San Antonio. The only route in those days was taking U.S. Highway 281 from San Antonio to Alice. In Alice he would take a right on Texas 44 and come chugging in on the last leg. I remember how beautiful the night was. We were on the courthouse grass, relaxing after a full day of running around town. We had been to the cave by the creek twice, early in the morning and in the middle of the afternoon. On the way in the afternoon, we had stopped at the creek and soaked our feet. We quickly got our feet out of the water when we saw a snake swim by, making Matías scream. It was an *alicante*, the dreaded hoop snake! But when we ran, it did not form into a hoop and roll and slash after us. Matías said the snake was water-logged and swollen and could not reach around to get its tail in its mouth to coil into a hoop, that the snake was somewhere close by watching us while it dried out, and that the minute it felt comfortable it would attack. We kept a wary eye out for it, but it never appeared. However, when it was time to leave, we went by way of the road and not the creek, adding a mile or so to our distance.

As we lay comfortably on the grass waiting for my grandfather, Juan began to tell us a story about a man who was hanged from the palm tree right above our heads. The man had gone crazy and killed his entire family—his wife and his three children—just because he did not like the way his wife was cooking supper. He described the way the man's body dangled, the rope around his neck, and how his legs shook and twitched. How the man's face turned blue and then purple, and how when he quit breathing they cut him down. We

listened carefully as Juan continued the story. There had
been a horrible mistake. The man was not dead. When they
were carrying him inside the courthouse, he revived and ran
away. They caught up with him and he cried out that he had
been hanged once and could not be hanged twice. The men
took him back to jail and he was retried again, this time for
trying to escape. He was hanged again and left to dangle
from the rope for two days to be sure he was dead. When the
sheriff and his men cut him down, he was still alive so they
put him in jail and never let him go. He was still in jail right
next to where we were sitting. If we looked carefully through
the bars, we might be able to see him inside his dark cell
looking out at us.

The stars were out in masses, so jumbled and close
together you could not possibly begin to count them. We were
so excited. We were going to beg our grandfather to take us to
Alice to walk around downtown. We enjoyed looking in at the
stores, looking at the displays in the windows. To us Alice,
Texas, was a metropolis.

At first we heard the faint rumblings of a car, but saw no
headlights. We sat up to listen. Juan had finished his story.
Then we saw the headlights flickering behind the dense
brush by the ditch on the curve of the highway. No one spoke.
We were praying that it be he, that he was safely home. The
car came slowly around the curve. The noise of the engine got
louder and louder. The outside wheels of the car were riding
on the shoulder of the highway. It had to be him. The car was
making more noise than on the Friday before. The car had
developed a hole somewhere in the exhaust.

We were waiting for him at the corner when we saw him
cautiously stick his arm out of the window to signal a left
turn. His was the only car on the road, and to see him signal
a turn caused us to start laughing. He turned, and we ran
next to the car. We could hear him laughing. Juan and
Matías jumped on the running board while the rest of us ran
behind the car.

"What is it now?" he asked as he struggled to get out of
the little car.

We followed him inside the house. My grandmother was
at the stove waiting for him. She and my grandfather
exchanged greetings as though he had never been gone. My
grandfather took off his hat and handed it to Matías. Then he

took off his coat and handed it to Frances. He sat down at the head of the table and we noticed under the naked kitchen bulb that his left eye was bruised. My grandmother wanted to know what had happened. He had been in a fight with a burglar at the liquor store on East Commerce. My grandmother fretted for a while about the eye, checking it out under the light of the bulb. She wanted him to quit working at the liquor store. She thought it too dangerous. He would not change his mind. It was the only job he could find at the time.

"Maybe one of these days I can come back to Alice," he said.

"What about San Diego?" my grandmother wanted to know.

There was no work in San Diego.

We were beginning to get edgy. All this talk about the fight in San Antonio and about work was keeping us from approaching my grandfather about the trip to Alice. Then the opening came. My grandfather said he would try Alice once more. We wanted to go to Alice with him. Could we go tomorrow? We wanted to go to Alice tomorrow. We begged and begged. It had been almost two months since we had gone. He did not remember the exact time, but he agreed we had waited too long. We would go to Alice in the morning. We would take our grandmother and mother with us. Once there, we would drive by my father's work place to tell him we had arrived from the long ten-mile trip. My grandfather would have a chance to look for work.

We carried our bedding outside on the porch. We lay on our quilts listening to the grownups tell their stories. We heard the news of the day. Mercé came by drunk and sat down on the edge of the porch. He did not say anything for a long time. Soon we heard him start to mumble, and we all knew he was about to have a fit. He stood up, violently grabbed his ears, and started yanking on them as he ran off into the darkness. We could hear him cursing Mrs. Luby. Finally, my grandfather told the story of the fight with the burglar. My grandmother winced when he described how the burglar had held him down and hit him in the eye.

"Took all the money, too," he said.

"You're going to die at that hateful store," my grandmother said.

My father drove in from work, got out of the car, waved in our direction, and went inside to eat supper.

At first we had seen what looked like a firefly at a great distance, but then we could see it was the lit lantern, moving in the dark. It was Pepa walking toward us. She came and sat at the edge of the crowd, mumbling about not finding her family at all during the day.

"And did you look real close?" my grandfather humored her.

"Yes," Pepa complained, "but they were not to be found."

"Tomorrow you'll find them," said my grandfather.

We hardly slept after everyone was gone. Juan and Matías were wrestling. Cota was telling stories. Maggie was pretending that she was snoring heavily. Frances was singing. My brother and sister and I were over in a corner trying to sleep, but so excited about the next day that we couldn't.

My grandfather always woke up very early. He was up by four in the morning. By seven, he and my grandmother had cooked breakfast and eaten and were waiting for us to finish getting ready. We ate and then piled into the car. My grandfather started the engine and made this horribly loud noise. It was getting worse. My grandmother complained, but he ignored her. He could not afford to fix the car this month. My grandmother was about to say something, but my grandfather gave her the familiar look that meant he did not intend to discuss the matter anymore. His mind was set.

We had our first flat tire about two miles out of San Diego. Everyone had to get out of the car. My grandmother, my mother, and Sylvia stood under a mesquite tree while we worked. With our help, it took my grandfather thirty minutes to fix the hole in the tube and pump up the tire. The second flat occurred as we went into Alice. We were close by the garage where my father worked, so my grandfather kept on driving on the rim until we got there. He and my father fixed the flat in a short time. My father gave each of us a nickel. Now we were ready to go to town.

We drove through Main Street, past all the stores with their wares displayed in the windows. It was an exciting time for us just to look around. It was a far cry from the cave and the creek and the dusty streets of San Diego. The car was creating such a noise that the people on the sidewalk shopping were staring at us. My grandfather stuck his arm out the window and bent his elbow, pointing his hand straight up. He turned right, past the J. C. Penny store and parked against the building. He switched the motor off and the abrupt end to the noise came as a pleasant respite. It would take our ears several minutes to clear the ringing. We could feel the easing of tension inside the car. My grandmother let out a sigh. She opened the door and said, "What a torture this has been. I could have stayed in the kitchen and had more fun."

My mother said, "At least we're here."

We were anxiously waiting for my grandfather's response, but he chose to ignore my grandmother. We were relieved. The last thing we wanted was an argument to ruin our trip. My grandfather ordered everyone out of the car. By this time my grandfather was standing on the sidewalk ready to go. We all gathered around him, took a left, and started our familiar walk on the south side of Main Street. We normally walked the three or four blocks to where the stores ended. Then we would cross the street and come back on the north side. All of this would take about an hour, maybe more if my grandmother or mother saw something they needed to buy. In that case, the two would run back and forth from one side of the street to the other comparing prices. Finally, a decision would be made to buy or not to buy. Then it was back to the car and the drive home.

We crossed the street to the north, and we came to the Traveler's Hotel where my grandfather had worked once. Next to it was the City Cafe where El Negro Joe had worked. My grandfather went in while we waited to ask for Joe.

"No one knows anything," he said. "They say he left Alice to go back to the old farm."

"Poor thing," my grandmother said.

My grandfather went into the Traveler's Hotel. We stayed outside, looking through the window while he went in and asked if there was a job available. We saw him shake hands with an old gray-haired man working the front desk. The man reminded us of Mr. Gallagher, but then, to us, most of the *gringos* looked alike. It appeared they knew each other. They spoke back and forth animatedly for a few moments. Then we saw the man shake his head. There were no jobs. My grandfather came out and said there was a possibility. To my grandfather there was always a possibility. My grandmother said that that meant there was no job. My grandfather shrugged his shoulders and said there might be one in the future.

We were walking by the barbershop when we saw a *gringo* boy about Matías' or Juan's age walk out sporting a nice looking haircut. He did not look as if someone had used a bowl for a template on his head like *Tío* Pacho had done to Juan. Matías and Juan strayed off and went into the barbershop, something we knew better than to do. My grandfather had gone into the hardware store next door to ask for a job. My grandmother and mother were ahead of my grandfather, looking through the window at the new fabrics. We panicked, and some of us went into the hardware store to look for my grandfather, and some went for my grandmother and mother. My grandfather was asking the manager for a job when we ran inside. We hated to interrupt him, but we had to. Matías and Juan were in the barbershop. My grandfather excused himself and ran out. He met my grandmother and mother out on the sidewalk. They could not believe Juan and Matías had gone inside the barbershop. My grandmother and my grandfather whispered. My grandfather hurried to the barbershop. The rest of us children were outside the barbershop door waiting to see what would happen. Matías and Juan had sat down as though they wanted a haircut. They were watching the barber cut another young man's hair. My grandfather went past us inside. By this time the barbershop owner had motioned to another barber, and he went for Matías and Juan. He asked them if they were Mexicans and they said yes. He picked them up by the shirt collar to throw them out. No Mexicans were allowed in an Anglo barbershop in Alice, and those were the only kind of barbershop on Main Street.

My grandfather stopped the barber and asked him to release the two boys. The barber shoved my grandfather aside. His hat flew off. His bruised eye was now showing. He staggered and fell down on one of the chairs. The rest of the men who had been kibitzing at the barbershop had long ago stopped to see what was going on. They had seen Matías and Juan come in and had wondered what Mexican children would be so brazen as to walk in. They saw my grandfather wrested by the barber. Now my grandfather was trying to get up from the chair. The men were up and walking toward him. They intended to throw him out. Matías and Juan came flying out of the barbershop, landing on the sidewalk. The barber who threw them out cleaned his hands. We all quickly went to help them up. My grandfather managed to get up and walk out before the crowd of men got to him. The hat came flying out, and the older barber, the one who owned the shop, came out and said, "Don't you ever show your face around here again." My grandfather picked up the hat, dusted it, and put it on his head.

We walked as fast as we could without running. We looked back and saw the empty sidewalk. The men were back inside the barbershop. We crossed the street across from J. C. Penny and got in the car. On the way home, my grandfather finally spoke. Why had Matías and Juan gone into the barbershop? They had wanted to see how the man cut hair so they could show *El Pequeño*, our barber in San Diego, how to do it.

"For a haircut, you nearly got us in trouble," my grandfather said.

"That's why I never like to go to Alice," my grandmother said.

"Nonsense," my grandfather scolded her, "it's good for the children."

"This is why I like San Diego," my mom said. "There the Mexican rules. Let them come here and try to push us around."

"In San Diego," my grandfather thought out loud, "a man like the barber would last ten minutes alive."

"Less," my grandmother corrected him.

Halfway to San Diego, we had our third flat, and we were so angry we didn't stop. Besides, we had run out of patches. We made it on the rim, creating a beautifully patterned set of white parallel lines on the asphalt all the way home.

Saying Goodbye

Tía Herminia came one Sunday from San Antonio. She was driven by her son Manuelito, a tall, handsome man in his early forties who always wore a suit. He was a taxi driver in San Antonio, and my grandmother admired him greatly. *Tía* Herminia was a fortune teller in San Antonio. She read fortunes in cards.

We were sitting outside when they drove up. At first, we did not recognize the car, bright and shiny and new. We walked over to see who it was, and instantly, we recognized the loud happy voice. She was having difficulty getting out of the car.

"I've been sitting too long," she explained as she laughingly stuck her hand out for us to give her a lift.

She was a heavy-boned lady, tall, full bodied, with very large feet. She laughed out loud when it took several of us to help her out of the car. Manuelito had come around to help, but he was too late. We had hold of both her hands and arms, and we were pulling her out. Along with *Tía* Herminia came a collection of empty bags of chips, cookies, and peanuts which she had been eating on the way. She was embarrassed to see the debris of food bags which fell to the ground by the car door.

Manuelito was anxiously reaching over us to help us get his mother out of the car.

"I am a big woman. Big bones," she said.

My grandmother had come out by then and was looking from the porch to see who it could be.

"Herminia!" she shouted upon recognizing the stout lady. "Blessed are these eyes that see you. Where have you been? What are you doing in San Diego?"

"I bring news," she said, now out of the car and dusting herself. "I bring news for my favorite cousin, María Saenz."

"Come in, for heavens sake," my grandmother said.

We were standing around the kitchen table watching *Tía* Herminia and Manuelito eat when she paused and said, "The truth is that I have some very bad news."

"Not Gonzalo," my grandmother said, referring to my grandfather who was still working in San Antonio at the liquor store.

"Oh, no," she said. She picked up her purse off the floor and opened it. She began to look for something. Manuelito, who traveled everywhere with his mother, knew what she was looking for. He reached into his back pocket and pulled out his handkerchief. He handed it to her, and she inspected it before wiping her hands.

"You have bad news?" my grandmother asked.

"Yes," she said, giving the handkerchief back to Manuelito. "I've come to tell you that Manuel died."

"Manuel, your husband?" my grandmother asked.

"Yes," *Tía* Herminia replied.

"*Ave María Purísima*. When did this happen?"

Tía Herminia felt bad for some reason. When she opened her mouth, we knew why.

She said, "Day before yesterday."

We all gasped. What was she doing here? We were famous for long wakes and funerals which lasted for days. My grandmother seemed bemused, as though she thought *Tía* Herminia was pulling her leg. A smile broke over her face.

"You're up to your old tricks," she told *Tía* Herminia.

"This time," she said, "I speak the truth. Manuel died day before yesterday."

My grandmother asked, "Day before yesterday? So soon ago?" She looked at us and said, "Go get Marillita."

We ran next door to get my mother. By the time we returned, *Tía* Herminia was on her second plate of *fideo* and beans. Manuelito was either tied or ahead one plate.

Tía Herminia made a great show when she saw my mother. She embraced her for a long time, talking at the same time, asking her if she remembered how my mother and Manuelito used go out walking in the morning to buy milk. For some reason this remembrance always caused her great joy. "Manuelito loved you so much," she said to my mother, "but you two are cousins. What bad luck Manuelito has with women."

"Manuel died?" my mother asked her.

"Yes," *Tía* Herminia replied, settling down. "Like I was telling your mother, María, he died day before yesterday. Manuelito and I are going from town to town informing the relatives."

"And why didn't you tell us before so we could go to the funeral?" my grandmother wanted to know.

"It happened so fast," *Tía* Herminia explained.

"Death is always fast," my grandmother said.

"Not this fast," *Tía* Herminia corrected her. "He was struck by the train coming home."

"Drunk," my grandmother surmised.

"You have always been very astute," *Tía* Herminia complimented my grandmother. "Anyway, Manuelito and I decided not to make too much of it. We talked it over and decided that the expense of a funeral would be too great. So we buried him right away. Yesterday, to be truthful, and we saved quite a bit of money. Nobody liked him, María. Who would have come to the funeral? Just a few of his drunken friends, that's who."

"We would have gone," my grandmother said.

Tía Herminia said, "Why bother you and Marillita? You have things to do. Other worries."

"Nothing would have prevented us from going to be with you in your hour of need," my mother said. "You must feel horrible."

"No, no, no," *Tía* Herminia said, almost cackling. "As a matter of fact, I feel wonderful. You don't understand the load that has been lifted from my back. The scorpion that has been removed from my backside."

"He was not a very good man," my grandmother said.

"Now we can say it without any fear of harm," *Tía* Herminia said seriously.

My mother, always one to deal in understatements, said, "He was a formidable man."

"Yes, he was," Tía Herminia declared. "You remember what a terrible person he was. Ask Manuelito."

"He was very mean," Manuelito agreed with his mother. "With me, he was very mean," he continued.

"That's enough, Manuelito," *Tía* Herminia scolded him. "Anyway, with what we saved on the funeral we're going to Hawaii."

"Where's that?" my grandmother asked.

"An island, María," *Tía* Herminia said. "Very far away. We're going by boat."

"From San Antonio?" Juan inquired.

Tía Herminia let out her laugh. "How ignorant you children are," she said. "No. Manuelito is driving me to Los Angeles and from there we take the boat.

"And where is Los Angeles?" Cota asked.

This brought on the loudest laughter of the day. Both *Tía* Herminia and Manuelito could hardly contain themselves.

When they were through laughing at us, *Tía* Herminia gave Manuelito the prearranged eye and they both stood up to leave. My grandmother would have none of that. They insisted on leaving. They began their farewell in the kitchen. *Tía* Herminia acted as though she insisted on leaving. My grandmother acted as though she would not let her leave.

"You can't leave," my grandmother said. "You just got here. You must spend the night."

"It's impossible, María," *Tía* Herminia said. "We have so many more people to see. We are going to Benavides and from there north to Freer. From Freer we may go to Laredo to eat goat. No. No. We have too much to do. Come, Manuelito. Help me to the car."

"But we haven't talked," my grandmother complained. "We haven't talked of anything yet. Nano was here."

"How is Nano?"

"Fine."

"We'll look him up in Laredo," *Tía* Herminia said to Manuelito.

Manuelito nodded. "Yes. That would be fine," he said.

Tía Herminia was embracing my grandmother for the longest time. "You know how much I love and appreciate you," she said. "Wait until Gonzalo dies. Maybe then you can get out of this house."

Manuelito looked at his watch. "It's time to go, mother," he said.

"See?" *Tía* Herminia declared, erupting with laughter once more. "See how Manuelito takes care of me? He's like a hen with me. Won't let me out of his sight." She stuck her hand in front of my grandmother and said, "Look at the ring he bought me. See?" She showed the pretty ring around.

My mother said, "How beautiful. It's so bright."

"Pure gold and a diamond," said *Tía* Herminia.

My grandmother remembered another excuse for them not to leave. "You didn't tell us our fortune. How can you leave without telling us our fortune?"

"The next time, María," *Tía* Herminia said.

"I insist you stay," my grandmother said.

"Oh, no, María," *Tía* Herminia uttered. "We do have to leave. And Manuelito has to drive his taxi day after tomorrow. You know how hard he works to keep his mother in diamonds."

She thought this remark to be one of the funniest she had ever heard. She was rocking on her large feet, laughing, her belly quivering.

Manuelito straightened out proudly. "I always think of my mother," he said.

"Oh, that my children were like that," my grandmother lamented. "See," she said to us, "see how a child is supposed to treat his mother?"

"We're leaving," said *Tía* Herminia, and she went for the door. Manuelito was right behind her. "Some other time, maybe after Hawaii, María, we'll come and stay for a few days. Manuelito and I will take you in his new car to Laredo. Maybe see Nano."

"Nano doesn't live at the same place," my mother warned them.

She said, "I know. He wrote and told me how all of you ate and stayed at the wrong house."

They were at the door and my grandmother and *Tía* Herminia embraced once more.

"You don't know how sorry I feel for Manuel. Poor soul. May God have him in His kingdom," my grandmother said.

"Never," *Tía* Herminia laughed.

"Now, mother," Manuelito said.

The whole group, we children included, was stacked at the kitchen door. The two older women were still embracing. Manuelito was next to them trying to reach behind them for the door handle.

"I'm doing so well," *Tía* Herminia told my grandmother, who was crying again.

Manuelito managed to reach the knob and opened the kitchen door. Both my grandmother and *Tía* Herminia spilled out onto the porch. We were slowly following them. They embraced once more at the porch, kissing each other on the cheek. When they were through telling each other how much they loved one another, they walked down the porch steps, their arms locked. Manuelito was holding on to his mother, making sure she did not fall. *Tía* Herminia looked nonchalantly at us, like a queen being helped down the stairs by an insignificant footman. My grandmother was having a difficult time taking the steps, trying to hold on to *Tía* Herminia. *Tía* Herminia scolded Manuelito for not helping my grandmother. "After all," she said, "María is the oldest." And that brought out so much laughter from her that she had to stop and take several breaths. At the bottom of the steps they embraced again and began another conversation about how Manuel had died.

Tía Herminia said, "I told you it was the train. He was coming home drunk and he walked into the train. They say he never heard it or saw it. Never knew what hit him. Manuelito says that we may collect some money from the train company. If we do, I'll let you know. Or I'll come over and show you some more diamond rings and furs. Oh, you must see Manuelito's new car. Come with me. Children," she said to us, "you can look, but please be careful."

It was a beautiful car, brand new. It smelled new. Manuelito stood at the driver's door like a chauffeur in the movies. He waited patiently for *Tía* Herminia to show my grandmother and mother all the gadgets inside.

"And look at this," she said, taking out the cigarette lighter. "This is to light your cigarette. But Manuelito doesn't smoke. I won't let him. Right, Manuelito?"

Manuelito said, "Yes."

"Oh, God has blessed me with such a beautiful son," *Tía* Herminia cried out. "The curse He placed on me with the husband He gave me, He more than made up for with my son. How fortunate I have been in that respect. Now we must go."

My grandmother and *Tía* Herminia embraced again, my grandmother still crying over Manuel's death. My mother was next in line to be hugged.

"How is Mercé?" *Tía* Herminia asked.

"He's fine, the scoundrel," my grandmother replied. "You know how he is."

"Someday they'll find a cure for him," she said. "They always do. Just you wait, and then all of you won't have to suffer with him. And Pepa?"

My grandmother made a face and said, "She should be coming by soon. She normally comes by in the early afternoon."

"And how is she?"

"Crazy."

"Well, what can you expect. It runs in the family," she said, and then laughed with so much enthusiasm that she had us laughing, too. "You know we come from crazy people, don't you, María?"

"It seems we have more than our share," my grandmother admitted amidst her laughter.

Tía Herminia said, "You remember the crazy things we used to do when we were children, don't you, María?"

My grandmother blushed. "Don't say anything," she cried out. "The children will hear."

"We were crazy then," *Tía* Herminia told us.

"Yes, we were," my grandmother remembered.

"Come, Manuelito, it's time to go."

Manuelito got in the car. My grandmother was holding on to *Tía* Herminia. "Must you leave so soon?" she pleaded.

"Yes," *Tía* Herminia said. "It's going to be late soon, and Manuelito doesn't like to drive on the roads at night. You never know the drunks that are out on the road. He drives a taxi and doesn't like to drive on the roads. Can you believe that? Manuelito is very particular, María. He doesn't even drive on the east side of San Antonio. It's horrible over there."

"That's where Gonzalo works," my grandmother said.

"Poor thing. All that crime. Manuelito says he wouldn't be caught dead in that part of town."

"Well, what can Gonzalo do?" my grandmother said.

"What time is it, Manuelito?" his mother asked him.

Manuelito looked at his wrist watch and said, "Five thirty."

"It's too late to leave," my grandmother said. "Five-thirty. Then it's six-thirty and then seven-thirty and then eight-thirty. You'll never make it."

"Is it really that late?" Tía Herminia inquired. "Is it really, really that late. Five-thirty?"

Manuelito said, "Yes, mother. It's five-thirty. A little after five thirty, if you want to be exact."

"A little after five-thirty, he says," Tía Herminia said. "Manuelito? Manuelito? Listen to me. You are not to drive in the night. You know how it offends you and scares you. I insist we stay overnight. Now, don't say anything against your mother because for sure God will punish you. Remember your father. You wouldn't want to be like him, now would you?"

"No," replied Manuelito. He was getting out of the car.

"Then get the bags out of the trunk," Tía Herminia said. "We are staying, and that is that. I want no argument from you, Manuelito. Look at how obedient he is, María. María, it's your fault. I always have such a good time with you that time seems to fly by. It's past five-thirty. We would never make it."

"I knew it," my grandmother said. "Didn't I tell you to stay the night?"

"You are such a dear, María," Tía Herminia said.

We took Tía Herminia and Manuelito to the Cotton Fiesta in Manuelito's new car. My grandmother and Tía Herminia and Manuelito were playing *lotería* when one of Tía Herminia's distant cousins recognized her. Quickly, between games, she came over to say hello and asked for her husband, Manuel.

"He's fine," Tía Herminia replied, preoccupied with winning her game. "He's resting comfortably."

"What else could I have said?" she asked my grandmother and mother afterwards. We were all laughing with her. "It was such a surprise, I didn't know what to say."

"You did the right thing," my grandmother said.

The next day's goodbyes took longer than the first. It began in the bedroom where Tía Herminia had slept. From there we went into the living room where she played the piano and we all sang. After eating, she and Manuelito took a short nap because Manuelito needed time to digest his food. If not, he would fall asleep at the wheel. When Manuelito awoke, we had pastry and coffee. But that did not seem to affect his digestion.

The goodbyes continued from the living room into the kitchen. At the porch there was renewed conversation about

Mercé, Pepa, Nano, Juanito Everett, *Tío* Pacho, Adolfo Arguijo, and my grandfather in San Antonio. *Tía* Herminia promised to go look my grandfather up and tell him hello for us. We wanted to know when was he coming home. "If Manuelito will drive me into that horrible part of town," she promised to go see him.

"Give him our love," my grandmother said.

"He will receive it," said *Tía* Herminia.

Just then, Pepa appeared from the backyard, having jumped the fence. She carried her lantern. *Tía* Herminia saw her at the same time we did and hurried to Pepa to embrace her. Pepa did not recognize her. *Tía* Herminia talked to her very gently and asked her how she was? Pepa kept asking us who the tall lady with the big feet was? *Tía* Herminia reached into her purse and took out a dollar bill and gave it to Pepa. They both walked over to where we stood by the car.

My grandmother and *Tía* Herminia embraced in the middle of the yard and again just before getting into the car. Once inside, *Tía* Herminia rolled the window down to talk some more. My grandmother and then my mother stuck their heads inside the car and kissed her. My mother came around and hugged Manuelito. He was very surprised. He wasn't used to being touched by women.

Tía Herminia said something about my grandmother going with them, and my grandmother thought about it and asked my mother. My mother didn't know. It was up to my grandmother to make up her mind. She hesitated.

"Should I?" she asked us.

We didn't want her to go. San Antonio was too far for her.

"It's better if I stay," my grandmother told *Tía* Herminia.

Tía Herminia kept insisting. "Come with me, María," she said. "Look at all the things we can do in San Antonio. We can go see Gonzalo. See how he's doing. Won't he be surprised?"

My grandmother said, "Would you wait for me to get ready?"

Tía Herminia said, "Sure, we can wait. Manuelito doesn't mind if I don't. It won't take you long."

My grandmother walked toward the house. "I don't know," she said. "I don't know if I should go. Gonzalo is not here to help me make up my mind."

"Forget about Gonzalo," *Tía* Herminia said from the car. "Just go in and get your things. Manuelito and I will wait for you. The trip will do you good. How can you stand to be stuck in the house all the time?"

My grandmother went into the house, and we followed her. She and my mother started to take out her clothes and then, suddenly, as suddenly as she had made up her mind to go, she had a change of heart.

"I'm not going," she said, sitting down on the bed. "How foolish of me to even think about it."

"Whatever you want," my mother said. "I thought you wanted to go."

"No, I didn't," my grandmother said. "I just had a wild dream, that's all. I don't know what got into me. How could I ever leave all of you?"

So back out we came, my grandmother up front to tell the waiting *Tía* Herminia that she would not go. *Tía* Herminia was so disappointed. She had already made two days worth of plans. Manuelito started the car and backed up. *Tía* Herminia was shouting about coming back soon to tell us our fortune. She would write from Hawaii.

"Who was that?" Pepa asked as we stood out on the street waving at the car.

My grandmother, of course, always wanted us to be like Manuelito, someone who could take her to Hawaii and buy her diamonds.

"You won't even go to San Antonio and you want to go to Hawaii," my mother told her.

"I could have gone," my grandmother said, "if I didn't have so many people to take care of."

My mother said, "You could have gone. We can take care of ourselves."

"If I left for a day," my grandmother said, "I would return to find all of you full of worms."

Christmas

Christmas was the time for excitement in all of our lives. Everything was anticipation. My grandfather loved the season as did my grandmother. He would be sure to take his vacation in the middle of December to spend the time with us. This year he wrote from San Antonio to tell my grandmother when he would arrive. It was his way of telling us to be at the courthouse on that night to greet him when he arrived in his old car. My grandmother and mother, with our help, would make tamales for several days. On the first night we would have a contest to see who had eaten the most. Whoever had the most empty corn shucks on the plate won. My father would bring the Christmas tree he had painted at the Chevrolet place where he worked and the whole house smelled of car paint. Mom would fix her favorite—fruit cake. She loved egg-nog. What would Santa Claus bring Juan and Matías and Cota and Maggie and Frances? At our house, we were arguing by the first of the month. Sylvia wanted a life-sized doll house. Richard wanted a doctor's bag just like the one Dr. Dunlap carried around on his house calls. I wanted a horse and boots, chaps and a hat, and a saddle, not the fancy one but the plain one in Sears Catalog. And if I couldn't get that, I wanted carpenter's tools to remodel Sylvia's doll house. At night, the three of us in bed together tried to outdo each other with our prayers. In the next bedroom, we could hear our father snoring.

Father Zavala made it special, too. This was the only time of the year when he personally selected his altar boys to serve during the holidays. His criteria for judging was stiff. He examined each of us and measured our Latin response for each Catholic ceremony. He wanted everything perfect.

"Dominus vobiscum?"

"Et cum spiritu tuo," came the immediate reply.

Faster. He wanted the response faster. "Place more emphasis into the response," he would say. "Mean it!"

"Sequentia sancti Evangelii secundum ..."

"Gloria tibi, Domine."

Matías was the best one for answering the priest in Latin, but unfortunately, he was the one who cursed the most, making him, according to Father Zavala, very unreliable. Who knew at what moment, if under duress, Matías wouldn't start cursing? Once, he stepped on the hem of his cassock while moving the giant missal from one side of the altar to the other, and he tripped. Before he touched the ground, he let go of the missal and as as he fell let out a stream of curse words which negated the whole Mass. We, including Father Zavala, could see our prayers heading downward instead of to Heaven.

We knew we didn't stand a chance, but we went and tried anyway. Father Zavala was standing in front of the altar, and one by one he called on us to respond to his words. We all faltered within moments of kneeling in front of the priest, except for Matías. He could answer as fast as the priest could think. But to no avail—Matías was distracted by movement in back of the altar. The sexton was sweeping cobwebs off the windows with a long broom, and Matías saw a spider fall on top of the man's head.

"¡A la chingada!" Matías cried out.

What a beautiful job the sexton and the housekeeper had done with the church. The Nativity scene to the left of the altar was stuck against the wall, the craggy paper painted rock-like. The crevices were laden with sheep, shepherds, and little children of different sizes, some bigger than the sheep, others smaller. The Christ child was huge compared to Joseph and Mary, but that was the way it was every year and no one questioned it. The Baby Jesus was larger than some of the cows in the manger, His little chipped feet and hands sticking skyward. We stopped to admire once more this work of art.

It was during practice in church one afternoon that we learned of the deformed baby born to a lady who lived by the creek. The baby was not yet a week old when the baby became seriously ill. Dr. Dunlap could not guarantee the health of the child. The parents wanted the child baptized. Dr. Dunlap didn't want the baby moved in the cold weather, so he asked Father Zavala if he could go baptize the baby at home. Father Zavala sent word to us that he needed help. We went with Father Zavala, trudging behind him, helping him carry the holy water and the sacred vessels. We were complaining about being interrupted from our play.

"This is the Lord's work," he said, looking back at us trailing behind, loaded with this paraphernalia.

When we got there, the parents were around the child, feeling helpless. We could see the child had one normal ear and one good eye. The other eye was a blur of skin. The side of his head where the other ear should have been was blank, a sheet of skin covering the ear hole. Dr. Dunlap who had done the delivery had said he had never seen a child with so many deformities. Who knew how many other abnormalities lay under the blanket which covered him?

On the afternoon of Christmas Eve, Father Zavala read out the names of the four altar boys who would serve him during the holidays. None of us had made the list. We went out to play in the park. Dr. Dunlap drove by with Clementina, the nurse, at his side. We knew he was going to see the baby, and we ran after the car. He went straight for the creek and then turned left at the street which paralleled the creek. He had left us behind, but we could see where he was going. Finally, he stopped by the house where the baby lived. By the time we arrived, Dr. Dunlap and Clementina were inside tending to the baby. We could see the doctor and the nurse and the parents inside. Closer and closer we came to the window. We could hear Dr. Dunlap speaking, trying to talk to the parents in Spanish.

Clementina spoke. In Spanish, she said, "The doctor says that the baby needs special milk. The baby cannot take mother's milk or cow's milk."

"Why?" the mother asked.

Dr. Dunlap said, "Tell her it's an allergy. It is not unusual."

"We have tried goat's milk," the father said to Clementina.

"And not even that works?" Clementina asked.

"No," the mother said. "It's all the same."

On the way out, Dr. Dunlap and Clementina saw us standing by the car. Dr. Dunlap greeted us and asked us what we were doing? We had come to see what was wrong with the baby.

"He can't eat," he said. "He cannot digest milk. The child is allergic to different types of milk." To Clementina he asked, "What about donkey's milk? Could we get some?"

"I don't know for sure," said Clementina. "There's usually a herd of donkeys close to town. Do the children know?"

We knew where a herd of donkeys had been grazing by the creek at the edge of town. But that had been in November. We had played with the donkeys, chasing them, trying to ride them. Matías had managed to get on one, and the donkey had reached around and bit him.

Dr. Dunlap went inside and came out with the baby's father. Dr. Dunlap asked if we could take the man to where we had last seen the donkeys.

"We can take him," Cota said, "but they're hard to catch."

The father said, "I can catch a donkey. I know how."

Dr. Dunlap said, "Well, it's worth a try. If not, the baby's not going to make it."

The father said to us, "Wait here," and he went inside the house.

Dr. Dunlap and Clementina left in his car. They had someone else they had to see.

The father came out with a burlap bag tied around his neck, draped around his chest. In it he had some dried ears of corn. He held a short rope in his hand. He was short and wiry, and acted as if he knew about horses, cows, and donkeys. He was all business and didn't say a word. We had never seen him in town before. He must have just moved from a ranch into town.

"What if they're not there?" Matías asked the father.

"I'll find them," he answered, "even if it takes the rest of my life."

We were disappointed when we got to the old pasture. The donkeys had moved on. The father started looking around, checking for any tell-tale signs on the ground. He appeared to have found something, and he started off moving away from town. We were now on a hilltop, and in the late afternoon we could look at the town spread out down below. The church spire, the only tall structure, stood out. Inside,

Father Zavala was practicing with his altar boys. On the other side of the hill, we could see the little valley and the donkeys grazing. The father had found them and gone ahead. When he was halfway down the hill, he stopped and waited for us.

He said, "Do not scare them. Do not act like you want to catch them. Look the other way. Do not run after them. Do not do anything. I will catch one. All I need is for you to circle the herd, but without forcing them together. Let them have their freedom. The minute they feel insecure, they will run. We don't want them to run."

Quietly, we crept up to the herd. The father was looking for a female with milk. Juan and Matías had gone around to encircle the donkeys from the opposite side. We were afraid of spooking the animals, so we stayed with the father. The donkeys had not sensed our presence yet. We crawled on all fours as close as we could get.

"Do not look the donkey in the eye," the father whispered. "If the donkey looks at you, look the other way. Act as if you do not see the animal."

Very slowly, the father stood up and the donkeys turned to look at him. He looked away. We all stood up when we saw him stand up. He took the bag of corn, shook it, then very quietly began scattering corn on the ground. The leader of the herd slowly came forward and sniffed the corn. Then it began to eat off the ground. The others followed his lead. Soon the small herd of donkeys was eating placidly. The man moved slowly and quietly among them without touching them. He was looking for udders with milk. When he found one, he slowly placed the rope on the donkey's back, barely touching it. The donkey looked back at him, and he looked away to the fading horizon. He slithered the rope up and down its back until the donkey paid no attention to what he was doing. Gradually he stepped forward, toward the animal's head, sliding the rope on the donkey's back. Before the donkey knew it, the man was standing at its neck, the rope dangling over it. Very gently and with very slow motion, he bent his knees and was able to reach under the neck and grab the rope. He tied a knot in the rope, slipped it over the neck once more, and tied it again. Not one donkey had moved other than to eat the corn. We were amazed at how capable a man who knew his way among animals could be. How different from us who chased the donkeys all over the brush.

The father enticed the donkey out of the herd by tying the bag of corn around her neck. As she tried to feed, she moved forward easily. Two other donkeys followed us. One was the young donkey, recently born, following his mother. The other, the man said, was the older daughter, not yet wanting to be weaned. Despite her age, she was already pregnant and ready to have milk.

On the way, nightfall came and we could see the stars. We had temporarily forgotten it was Christmas Eve until we reached the top of the hill. Below, we could see all the lights of the church lit. Father Zavala would be inside helping light the candles. There was a chill in the air now that the sun had set. We had all forgotten our jackets. Mom and grandmother would be angry. We would catch a cold and get pneumonia and get so sick we could die. The stars had begun to shine and we were looking for the brightest of them all to see if the Baby Jesus had been born. Juan saw the star, a beautiful star close to the moon and pointed it out to us.

"It's shining for us," said Frances. But we knew it couldn't be true.

The man was up ahead with the donkey and the two stragglers following him. Once we got to town we told him we were going home and he thanked us for telling him where the donkeys lived. He was new in town, he explained. "But now I know," he said.

Midnight Mass was beautiful. When the altar boy rang the bell and Father Zavala emerged from the sacristy, he almost took the congregation's breath away. He wore his most brilliant chasuble, perfectly white and trimmed in gold and red thread. The stole was a white cloth embroidered in green and red, his favorite Christmas colors. He looked magnificent, tall and erect and bathed, his white hair slicked back, moving about the altar with a great presence. It could not have been a more perfect Mass. For once, we were dumbstruck.

None of us got what we wanted for Christmas, but we knew all along we wouldn't. It was all make-believe: Sylvia's doll house. Richard's doctor's bag. My chaps and boots and horse. And we knew better than to be disappointed. Christmas Day would be another day full of wonder for us.

We would see about the dog and the donkeys. We would spend time with grandfather. We would visit Father Zavala, maybe play some baseball for him. We would get Mercé out from the beer joint to tell him it was time to eat. We would take a plate of food to Pepa, if she hadn't come by already. We would much rather have ourselves than toys. We could always make toys.

The baby thrived on donkey's milk. And when he grew up, the town nicknamed him *Leche de Burra*, Donkey's Milk.

I Can Hear the Cowbells Ring

As we usually did every two weeks or so, we were waiting at the courthouse yard on a Friday night for my grandfather to drive in from San Antonio. It was unbelievable how many stars we could see as we lay on our backs on the grass, passing a cigarette around. My sister Sylvia had just asked about clouds, and Matías, who thought he knew everything, was expounding on how clouds are made of smoke.

"I know that," said Frances, as ignorant as Matías. "But where does the smoke come from?"

"From people smoking," Matías replied. "From the wood burned in stoves."

There was a lot of smoke in South Texas. No rain. Just smoke.

Which reminded me to ask why it didn't snow in San Diego.

The standard answer from our elders, from the old codgers in town who hung around the pool hall all day, was that it was too cold to snow.

In the dead of winter when we went to bed, all of us in one bed to keep warm, we would pray for snow. In the morning, we would be disappointed. Why had it not snowed?

"It's too cold," my father would say, blowing on his hands to warm up.

Once it did snow, and I remember being sick with chicken pox and watching from inside at everyone playing in the snow, making snowballs and throwing them at each other. Juan brought a snowball in for me to hold. The others stood by my window watching to see how I would react to the coldness. Matías melted a snowball on the stove, thinking he would get milk.

"It's too cold for it to snow," said Maggie, echoing what we had heard so many times before.

We did not know it at the time, but my grandfather was coming home to stay. He had been assaulted one too many times at the liquor store in San Antonio, and my grandmother would not be letting him return.

There was no traffic on the road to Alice. The road was quiet and dark until my grandfather drove into view. From a distance of a few miles, we could see the headlights of his little car. We were sure it was him. He drove in slowly, as usual. No one ever drove as slowly as he did. Never in a hurry to get home. What had he brought us, we wondered.

At the cafe across the street from the courthouse, he turned toward home. We were waiting for him by the road by then. Again, Juan and Matías were fast enough to catch up with him and jump on the running board. My grandfather was laughing. Happy. Happy to be back with us.

At home, he hugged us all, one at a time. He felt, as always, so soft and tender. We had so many questions that he began to laugh at the hard time he was having trying to answer. We went searching through the car afterwards. Maybe he had brought something for us, something other than a goat. Of course, he had not brought anything. We knew it. It was all a game we loved to play. One day he would buy us something, we thought, and what a joy that day would be. But he never did. He barely had enough to keep the family fed.

My grandmother took a good look at him under the light bulb when he came in and said, "Take off your hat."

He took it off. Then, without the shadow from his hat, we could see the bruises on his face.

"Look at you," she said. "You are not going back."

"No," he said, sitting down to supper, "I'm not going back. This time I brought everything with me."

We were so happy to hear he was staying.

"If I knew who it was that beat you up," Juan said, "I would beat him up."

"Me, too," said Cota.

My grandfather smiled a painful smile. He said, "How green is your corn. This man was as big as a mountain."

"We don't care," said Matías. "We can whip anyone. All of us gang up on this man, and we take him by surprise. Maybe when it's real dark and he doesn't know we're following him. And then we strike. We grab him by the legs."

"By the arms," said Frances.

"We hit him on the head," said Maggie.

Matías was boxing around the kitchen, throwing jabs at the air.

My grandfather was laughing so much he could not chew. "You children talk a good fight," he said. "I'd like to see you in the heat of battle."

"They would run," said my grandmother.

We were not going to argue with my grandmother. We knew how useless that was, but we thought we could defeat any man alive. It was all a matter of planning.

In the morning we piled into the little car and drove off to Alice to see about trading the car for a truck. When we got to the garage, we could see the old Dodge truck my grandfather had used for so many years, the one he had traded for the car, the one without the doors. It was sitting at the rear of the lot, unsold. My grandfather was an expert at haggling for automobiles, and in an hour he had traded the car back for the truck, and he had made some money besides. We all climbed on the back of the truck and we went to see my father at work.

My father was painting a car when we arrived, so we had to wait for him to come out of the paint room. He came out, his face and arms colored in automobile red, wiping himself off with a rag dripping with paint thinner. As they checked the truck, my father agreed with my grandfather that the deal was a good one, getting the old truck back and some money besides.

By now we had gotten off the truck, and we, too, were inspecting it. My father and grandfather went under the truck to check it, and we squatted around the truck to peer underneath, to see what they were doing. We could hear them talking. They came out from under and walked over to the front of the truck. My grandfather opened the hood to reveal the engine with all its mysterious wires and pipes. All was in order. My grandfather made it a point to notice that the truck had not been driven five miles since he had traded it for the car, and those miles were from moving the truck from the back of the lot to the front, trying to sell it. The fact that no one else wanted the truck didn't matter to us. The truck was a lot more fun than the car. We could stand up at the back, on the bed, and wave at the world as we drove by.

My father brought out some cans of oil for an oil change, and along with him came a mechanic friend who for a pint of whiskey would finish checking out the engine and the transmission. The mechanic leaned under the hood with both his dirty hands on the fender. He remained quiet, listening to the engine run while we stood by him wondering what he was thinking. He appeared lost in concentration, taking in the noise of the engine, evaluating the insides like a doctor listening for signs of illness. He asked my grandfather to step on the pedal while he turned the little screws on the carburetor. He went under the truck with it still running, and we could see his hand sticking out, his thumb up, wanting my grandfather to accelerate the engine. The transmission sounded good. But to be sure, he needed to take it apart. No need for that. His word was good enough. After a while he stepped back to make his diagnosis. As he rubbed his chin he said it needed new plugs, a new rotor, and a new distributor cap. Aside from that, the truck was in good shape.

The mechanic took the pint of whiskey from my father. We were hoping he would stash it away in his pocket and walk off, but he uncapped it. His first mistake. He took a swallow and made a sour face. He passed the bottle to my grandfather who did not drink. The mechanic took the bottle from my grandfather and passed it to my father, who did. His second mistake. My father tipped and drank the whole bottle without taking a breath. We had seen him do it so many times that we knew it was coming. The mechanic cursed under his breath.

"Gonzalo," he said, walking away, "you're crazy. You know that? You're crazy."

My father said, grinning, "I need it to cut the paint in my blood."

That night we had a good time hearing stories. It was early springtime and my grandfather enjoyed sleeping out-side in a small folding bed under the salt cedars. There was only one unwritten law about the bed. He liked his bed cold, and he would not allow anyone, except himself, to sit and warm his bed. My grandmother, my mother, and my father were sitting in chairs. We were sitting on the dirt.

My grandfather told us how he had been assaulted, how the man had caught him by surprise when his back was turned.

"If you had known, you would have beaten him up, right father?" Juan asked.

Our hearts ached to imagine him, the head of this family, being so vulnerable.

He said, "I don't know, children. He was so big. He probably would have beaten me even if I had had a week's notice."

Mercé was there, leaning against a salt cedar, rolling a cigarette. He was acting nervous, mumbling about something, something bothering his mind.

"Are you all right, Mercé?" my grandmother asked him.

"Yes," he said.

"Are you drunk?" my grandfather asked.

"No," Mercé replied.

My mother said, "You ought to go to bed. You might be tired."

My father said, "Tired from what?"

"From hanging around the beer joints," my grandfather said.

My father asked him, "You brought the cow?"

He had. We had seen him bringing the cow in earlier, the cow leading him home.

Presently, Mercé said good night and left. We could see him walking to the corner where his house was, and before he got there, my grandmother said, "Watch. Just watch. He's getting ready to have a fit."

Mercé started running, throwing off his hat, pulling at his ears, cursing.

"I knew it," said my grandmother. She got up, walked out to the street and yelled out for him to be careful. The Lubys had put up a new barbed-wire fence. "All we need is for him to run into the fence overnight," she said.

We could see the lantern jumping the fences and we knew it was Pepa crossing backyards. She arrived winded and could hardly speak. She had seen her dead husband and children in the patch of mesquite near her house, and she had run to tell us that finally she would have her family with her.

"You know how they are," she said of them. "They tell me they're coming, but they never do. Just to make me cry."

No one bothered to tell her the truth. She took a seat by me on the ground, placing the lantern in front of her. Then she began to stroke my hair. I didn't want her to touch me. That's all it would take for the rest of them to make fun of me. My mother noticed my discomfort and said, "Leave the poor child alone, Pepa. He doesn't like to be touched."

"I touch him all the time," she said.

"Yes," my mother tried to explain, "but he doesn't like it."

"He likes it," Pepa insisted.

"Leave the poor child alone," my grandmother said.

"I always touch him," said Pepa.

"But not tonight," my mother said.

"Maybe he can sleep with me," said Pepa. "I need him to be there when the others return."

"He can't sleep with you, Pepa," my grandfather said. "He needs to sleep with his family. He doesn't need to be sleeping with crazy people."

Pepa was offended. She said, "I'm not crazy."

"Well," my grandmother said, "we're not going to argue that."

"Only to help me when the others return," said Pepa.

"All right," my grandmother said. "When the others return, he can go sleep with you. You tell us when the others return."

"Tomorrow," said Pepa, quickly.

"Well," said my mother, "tomorrow he can sleep with you."

My grandmother said, "But I don't want you to come here lying. If they return, we have to see them. If not, the child does not go sleep with you."

"I don't lie," Pepa said.

"Yes, you do," my grandmother said. "You lie all the time. Just yesterday you lied about the lantern."

"I forgot where I put it," Pepa explained.

"Why don't you forget about coming over to bother us?" my grandmother asked.

"That's fine," said Pepa. "Tomorrow, when they return, I'll bring them to show you. You just wait. Tomorrow."

Another uncle, Juanito Everett, came by, waiting for my grandmother to make him a fold-over with a tortilla and the supper meat and some potato. But first, to pay for the meal, he told us the stories of the day: the man who brought the eggs into town every day was sick from a rattlesnake bite. He had reached into the hen's nest under the house without looking and had grabbed a rattlesnake instead of an egg. A horse had kicked the farrier on the head and he was homebound. His wife was soaking his head wrapped in yards of torn sheets. The wife did not want Dr. Dunlap to know. She did not want Dr. Dunlap to send her husband to the hospital. One of the mules belonging to the house mover who didn't bathe, who instead anointed himself with mentholated petrolatum, had gone crazy and had dragged a timber used for moving houses through the center of town, damaging the barbershop porch. The man with the wheelbarrow, who scavenged the town for trash, was sick. No one knew what ailed him. Dr. Dunlap wanted to send him to Corpus Christi. But the wheelbarrow man would rather die than leave town. He was afraid to travel, afraid of cars. There were too many cars in Corpus Christi. Juanito Everett roamed the streets and gambled small amounts at night so he knew the stories. There was more: Father Zavala had ordered new vestments. Otilia, his housekeeper, had told Juanito Everett. The man who hated glass had broken the store window at Tío Amando's Meat Market for the third or fourth time. Tío Amando had chased him off with a meat cleaver, thrown it at him, and barely missed killing him.

My father said, "If Tío Amando had wanted to kill him, he would not have missed."

There were new verses written for the man running for County Judge against the incumbent. Juanito Everett recited the verses, in couplet. The verses were witty and we all laughed. Hoping he had entertained us enough to warrant another meal in the near future, he left with not one, but two fold-overs after shaking my grandfather's and my father's hand. He was not half a block away when my grandmother started laughing at him. He was an old cowboy who still wore his pant legs inside his boots. We could see the light from the lamp on the park shining through his legs. He looked like he had been born on a horse.

My grandmother said, laughing, "Juanito Everett is the most bowlegged person I have ever known."

"Not really," my mother said, "remember the sisters who live by the courthouse?"

"You're right," my grandmother remembered. "They are worse than Juanito. Worse, because they are women."

My grandfather said, "His mother carried Juanito straddled around her waist. That is why he's bow-legged. His mother never let him touch the floor until he was five. He never walked until he was six."

"That's a lie," said my grandmother. She knew when my grandfather was making up a story.

"It's the cowboy boots," my father said. "They'll bend a man's legs. Juanito has worn cowboy boots since he was a baby."

My mother said, "Wasn't he riding a horse at one?"

"Who was that?" Pepa asked. She had taken out a saltine cracker from her skirt and was chewing on it.

"Juanito," said my grandmother. "Your cousin."

"Who?" she asked again.

"Juanito," my father said loudly.

"I'm not deaf," said Pepa.

"Then why do you ask?" my grandmother asked her.

"Because I know they'll come," said Pepa.

"Everybody will be coming," my mother said.

Pepa said, "Really? That's nice to know."

"Don't carry on a conversation with her," my grandmother said. "Maybe if we ignore her she'll go away."

We could see Mercé off in a distance by the Luby house, still yanking at his ears and cursing.

"I hope he doesn't lose his hat," my grandmother said. "Before you children go to bed, I want you to go get his hat."

"Poor Pepa," my grandfather said. "Crazy. But at least she hasn't gotten worse. She's still the same crazy Pepa."

"I don't see how she can get worse," said my grandmother.

"She could be violent," my mother remarked.

"That's true," my grandmother agreed.

And Pepa looked at them as if they were talking of someone else.

Pepa turned to me and said, "I'm not deaf. Tell them I'm not deaf."

"She's not deaf," I said, and everyone started laughing.

"Don't pay so much attention to her," my grandmother said.

After Juanito Everett had disappeared into the night from which he came, the conversation turned to what my grandfather would do for a living.

"You can go back to Alice and sell cars," my grandmother said.

Mercé's fit had subsided.

"No," said my grandfather. "I have a job."

"I knew you had something," my father said. "Is that why you traded for the truck?"

My grandfather said, "Yes. That is why I traded for the truck."

My grandfather had his plans. His brother in San Antonio, who worked for Coca-Cola, had bought a small piece of land between San Diego and Freer. He asked my grandfather if he would work the land. They would go half and half.

My grandmother said, "That would be better than having you work in the liquor store. You'll be much safer."

We hated for the night to end. The conversation was so interesting. Where was the ranch? How many horses would we have? How many cows? Would we have goats?

"Will we have goats?" my grandfather asked, laughing at how silly the question had been. "You won't be able to count them."

Watermelons. Gourds like the ones we tried to grow at Mr. Gallagher's place. No hogs. We did not want hogs.

"It's too hot for hogs," my father said.

He'd plant sorghum so sweet, as sweet as sugar cane, corn so tender you'd eat it without cooking, and raw peanuts, which gave us diarrhea.

But my grandfather yawned and said, "It's time to go to sleep."

I hated to go to sleep. It was early. Pepa had dozed off in front of her lantern, a small piece of cracker stuck to her fingers. Mercé was walking calmly toward his house, ready for bed. He had found his hat and had it on. We would not have to go get it for him.

Cano, who worked for the Lubys, went by, and that meant the movie house had closed. He tipped his hat in our direction and said, "Good evening."

"*Buenas noches, Cano,*" we all replied.

Out of respect, so that he was sure we were not talking about him, we remained quiet until Cano had gone past. When he was out of hearing range, my grandmother reminded us that Cano was older than anyone thought.

My mother said, "Oh, Cano was Cano when I was little."

"He must be one-hundred years old," my grandmother said. "He was old when I was young."

"He's turned into stone," my father said.

And then someone asked my grandfather the favorite question. "Why don't you want María to sleep outside with you?"

"Because," said my grandfather, yawning again, "together we're too big. The neighbors will think we slaughtered hogs and didn't share pork skins and lard."

Very early the next morning we met my grandfather for breakfast. We were going with my grandfather to see about his brother's ranch. It was a very grown-up thing for us to do, to eat breakfast with my grandfather, to participate in the conversation. There would be goats to buy, cows, mules, maybe a horse, corn to be planted, watermelons, peanuts, sorghum. We were going to be farmers and ranchers. We could see the money coming in, finally. Finally, my grandfather would have money. The dreams became grandiose over breakfast despite warnings from my grandfather.

Matías got carried away. He wanted to ride the calves. He wanted to make them buck, just like the cowboys in the movies. Juan wanted to rope them off his horse. He would throw a lariat over their head, yank it tight, and the calf would hit the end of the rope and do a somersault. He would jump off his horse, hog-tie the calves, and brand them.

My grandfather got serious. He said, "I don't want to see any of you roping and riding a calf. Do you understand? That's a good way to ruin calves." He was mocking us, of course.

We apologized for being so mean to the calves.

The girls wanted to play with the baby goats. They wanted my grandfather to promise not to sell them. He promised he would not sell them. We could only have one billy goat because they smelled so bad. We didn't want to smell like a billy goat.

My mother and grandmother saw us off. I was the only one who was made to ride in the front seat with my grandfather. They decided I was too little to ride in the back. We would be going through some rough terrain. My mother and grandmother said that I could fall off the truck and no one would ever know.

"Be careful with him, Gonzalo," my mother said of me as they snuggled me against my grandfather.

Right outside of town we took the limestone road north, and a few miles later we had our first flat. That took half an hour for my grandfather to fix while we chased rabbits and roadrunners in the brush and cactus.

I loved riding with my grandfather because we would talk about many things. He didn't have to tell me how to live or how to behave. He assumed that being raised among Juan and Matías, Cota, Frances, and Maggie was enough to make me mind my manners. So we talked of things we saw as we rode: the land. He knew the different soils and what to grow in them. He knew where there was oil. The problem was that he didn't own the land. The countryside. He knew the name of every bush, every tree, every cactus. He knew the name of every bird. I thought he knew everything.

It was early afternoon and we still weren't there because my grandfather drove so slowly and he weaved from side to side as he spoke, waving his hands and throwing his head back when he laughed. I could hear the banging on the top of the cab from the crowd outside asking for more speed. But my grandfather ignored them.

"They don't know what they're missing going fast," he said. "You miss a lot of things you ought to see and enjoy."

We had not been told that there was no ranch house. There were some pens at the top of the hill, but that was all.

We got off the truck and ran to the empty pens. Then we ran around looking for the house we were to stay in.

"A good ranch," my grandfather said, "always starts from the ground up."

It was his way of saying we had to sleep on the truck for three nights while we helped him build a room from the small amount of lumber and the metal Coca-Cola signs his brother had left for us.

Besides having no house, we had no water well, so my grandfather had to find water at the next ranch five miles away. We would go every two days to fill a barrel of water which tasted like epsom salts and bring it back for us to drink. Then he got the idea that we were not strong enough to work the ranch, so he added iron nails, the ones we used to nail the lumber, to the water to help our strength.

He accumulated livestock gradually. We bartered for our first cow with the man who owned the ranch with the well. My grandfather would pay him off in watermelons. We brought the cow back tied to the truck, slowly making our way. We were able to barter for two goats and a billy goat with a promise to pay off in corn. Our uncle from San Antonio finally showed up with more lumber and old Coca-Cola signs, and we were able to enlarge the room. He also brought seed and money for us to buy a planter. But we had no mule. My grandfather bartered for a mule, and soon he was planting, late, but still in the spring.

Things were looking up for us. The most excitement we had was when the wind would blow at night, buckling and making the Coca-Cola signs vibrate. The sound was unbelievable, like hundreds of thunders going off at the same time. And then followed the silence of the night penetrated by the solitary cowbell dangling from the neck of the cow somewhere in the brush, its sound so interesting, telling us exactly what the cow was doing. Grazing, we could hear the slow steady beat as she bobbed her head tearing off grass. And then the sudden burst of sounds when something scared her and she ran off.

In the morning we would eat outside, sitting at the table on top of the hill, looking down at the dew-covered land. The cow ~~horse~~ and mule would call us. The goats would be anxious to graze the brush.

School reopened and all of them left us. My grandfather and I stayed behind. Suddenly, we were alone. We missed not having the whole group.

We spent the days and nights together, two lonely souls living on a desolate land, united, not by age, but by the common bonds of love and survival. We slept together, ate together, worked together, and watched out for each other. To him, I was a little man. Those were carefree days. Most important, I had him all to myself.

In the summer we were all back together again.

My grandfather bought the meanest billy goat we had ever known, and only my grandfather could control him.

When he left us alone to get water and went by himself, the billy goat attacked us, chased us all over the hill.

One day, when my grandfather was gone, we decided to teach the billy goat a lesson. We allowed him to chase us until he tired. Then we double roped him without any trouble. We snuggled him to a fence post and covered his face with a burlap sack so he wouldn't see what we were going to do to him. Juan volunteered to get on the billy goat's back. We tied Juan down after he sat on the billy goat. Then we turned the billy goat loose and ran. The billy goat bucked around the yard with Juan on his back. We were all screaming for Juan to stay on. The billy goat stopped after a good while of bucking, trying to get Juan off his back. He was panting. His tongue was hanging out of his mouth, his legs spread out as if he was going to collapse. Juan had had enough. He was trying to untie himself. But the billy goat was not about to fall, not this billy goat. His eyes bulged out as he took on a look of ferocity we had never seen, and he seemed to get angrier and draw a burst of new energy from his orneriness. He galloped off into the brush with Juan screaming for us to untie him. We could almost feel Juan's pain as we heard the slashing sounds of the brush against his body and the billy goat's. Juan returned later, most of his clothes torn off, his body scratched so badly that my grandfather almost didn't recognize him when he returned with the barrel of water.

"Is that Juan?" he asked as we helped him unload.

"Yes," we replied.

"What happened to Juan?" my grandfather asked.

Juan said, "I ran through the brush. I went crazy like Mercé."

"Is that why you smell like a billy goat?" my grandfather asked.

We didn't see the billy goat for a few days. When he returned, he still had the rope around his belly. He respected us from then on.

Every weekend we would go back to San Diego, arriving Saturday noon. We would go off to town, maybe sneak into a movie, acting like rich landowners while my grandfather went to the grocery store to buy food for the week. Sunday morning, we would be back on the truck.

Week by week we improved the house. My grandmother came to stay. She was very critical of the way we were living.

"Like animals," she said, "on a dirt floor."

She loved the ranch life. She brought two beds, and a wood burning stove with an oven. We didn't know my grandfather could cook, but he cooked the best beans and baked the best bread we had ever tasted. But then again, everything tasted better cooked with mesquite. We planted corn and watermelons and peanuts and sorghum. He bought two more milk cows, although we preferred goat's milk. We came to have many goats aside from the one mean billy goat.

Every animal we owned had a name, so it made it difficult to sell any of them. We all would cry when my grandfather loaded an animal for the sale barn. We mourned for days.

"We have to eat," my grandfather would explain. "We are not into this labor for sentimental reasons."

The cows were Precious and Beauty and Madam. Each one had her own cowbell, and each cowbell had a distinctive sound. In bed at night, my grandfather would say, "*La Preciosa* is by the pen looking for something to eat." Or,"*La Madama* is grazing very well tonight. She has found grass." A violent shaking of the cowbell and he would say, "Did you children hear that? *La Bonita* just smelled a snake."

We stayed at the ranch for a couple of years, and then the drought came. In an area where rainfall is precious, we were denied any at all. We lived in a cloud of dust. My grandmother went back to San Diego. She could not live with the dust. Gradually, we had fewer and fewer animals, grew fewer and fewer crops. Even the mesquite, whose roots grow deeper than its heighth, began to die. We cried when my grandfather had to sell the mean billy goat. We watched silently as the new owners roped him in the pen, dragged him to the back of the truck, and hauled him off, a look of bewilderment in his eyes, his four feet tied together. And still more wailing when the cows cried out for us not to let them go. Then the mule and the horse were gone.

My grandfather's brother asked us to leave. We lost everything. We had to move on. My grandfather returned to San Antonio.

We hated to leave. We hated to see my grandfather fail once more. It was another one of those unfulfilled dreams which linger forever in memories. And to this day, I can hear the cowbells ring.